W9-BZW-185

REFLECTIONS

THE HISTORY OF DISABILITY SERIES

GENERAL EDITORS: Paul K. Longmore and Lauri Umansky

The New Disability History: American Perspectives
Paul K. Longmore and Lauri Umansky

Reflections: The Life and Writings of a Young Blind Woman in
Post-Revolutionary France
Thérèse-Adèle Husson
translated and with commentary by
Catherine J. Kudlick and Zina Weygand

"Reflections on the Physical and Moral Condition of the Blind by Mlle Adelle husson, young blind woman of Nancy." Title page of the original manuscript.

REFLECTIONS

THE LIFE AND WRITINGS OF A

YOUNG BLIND WOMAN IN

POST-REVOLUTIONARY FRANCE

THÉRÈSE-ADÈLE HUSSON

TRANSLATED AND WITH COMMENTARY BY
CATHERINE J. KUDLICK AND ZINA WEYGAND

NEW YORK UNIVERSITY PRESS
NEW YORK AND LONDON

NEW YORK UNIVERSITY PRESS
New York and London

Library of Congress Cataloging-in-Publication Data
Husson, Thérèse-Adèle, 1803–1831.
Reflections : the life and writings of a young blind woman in
post-revolutionary France / Thérèse-Adèle Husson ;
translated and with commentary by Catherine J. Kudlick
and Zina Weygand.
p.   cm. — (The history of disability series)
Includes text of the author's Reflections and of her Note on the
author's youth.
ISBN 0-8147-4746-9
1. Husson, Thérèse-Adèle, 1803–1831. 2. Blind
women—France—Biography. 3. Blind—Conduct of life.
I. Kudlick, Catherine Jean. II. Weyagand, Zina. III. Title.
IV. Series.
HV1967.H87 H86 2001
362.4′1′092—dc21   2001003603

New York University Press books are printed on acid-free paper,
and their binding materials are chosen for strength and durability.

Manufactured in the United States of America

10 9 8 7 6 5 4 3 2 1

In memory of
Thérèse-Adèle Husson
(1803–1831)

Contents

ix

FOREWORD

BONNIE G. SMITH

"But what do I know about the history of the blind or, for that matter, blind people at all?" I wondered when I received an invitation a few years back to discuss a paper about Adèle Husson, whose 1825 "Reflections" and later "Note on the Author's Youth" you are about to read. There was the additional worry that these writings might not have all that much to offer because they came from someone whose experience of the world must surely have been limited by her blindness.

Oddly enough, these were precisely the responses people often directed against my own writing on women. What could studying women—so removed from power and influence—possibly have to teach us? Why read about someone new and different, far from my own knowledge, experience, and interests?

The eventual meeting with an obscure figure in history, Adèle Husson, and her very talented discoverers, Catherine J. Kudlick and Zina Weygand, opened my eyes to the exciting world of disability studies. This inter-disciplinary field, still in the making, takes the story of that bodily difference once called "handicap" beyond the domain of doctors and other caretakers writing about their patients. Instead, scholars, social commentators, and a range of blind, deaf, paraplegic, and other people whose bodies vary from what has been established as the "norm" have given fresh and challenging ways to understand human difference and "normalcy's" relationship to it. These writers and activists remove the story of disability from the realm of science and place it squarely in the world of cultural values, social rules, aesthetic norms, and economic systems—the very things at the heart of much exciting scholarship today.

One result is a new approach to literature, history, philosophy, and the arts that allows us to understand how memoirs, novels, works of art, and laws have insistently portrayed those with disabilities in ways that promote the importance of so-called normal people. Disabled characters in literature, for example, function to make sympathetic heroes more heroic and villains more villainous. The miser Scrooge in Charles Dickens's *A Christmas Carol* epitomizes wickedness because he harasses the family of the lame child Tiny Tim. In other cases villains are given disabled bodies as symbols of character flaws, thus making disability a sign of human depravity. Painting and film have depicted the horrors of war in the twentieth century by focusing on disabled bodies and mental impairments resulting from the experience of combat. Thus, far from being marginal to modern society, disabled people have been central to its most important intellectual projects—invisible but highly visible. We are reevaluating our culture as a whole because of disability studies.

This book of Adèle Husson's writings and the two

scholars' detective work that uncovered her intriguing story shows another and perhaps more important break-through of disability studies: a new value discovered in the writing, art, thoughts, and way of life of disabled people themselves. How far Husson's story appears from the portrayals of artists, writers, and social commentators, as she attempts to interpret for her readers the sensibility and inner life of a blind person. Instead of being rather vacant, as one sometimes supposes those without access to a full range of senses to be, Husson is full of ideas, an instructor trying to teach others not to treat blind people as fragile, partial, and without feeling, but rather to see them as full of capacity and sensibility. And here is one of many lessons one draws from her work: people with disabilities should not be objects, as science and other cultural values would have them, but subjects of their own stories and experiences. Husson proclaims the importance of bodily variety as well as her own perspective on her body and life as a blind person.

Husson also challenges the modern notions of citizenship and the relationships between the individual and the senses that emerged in the nineteenth century. Whereas modern citizens believed themselves to inhabit the realm of pure idealism and disembodied rationality, Husson provides a dignified, relentlessly physical self-description. She writes of stumbling feet, the blind person's carriage of the head, the relationship to friends not through visual scrutiny but through warm embrace and other tactile responses to human presence. Modern rationality is said to rest on the power of visual observation, with hearing and touch secondary qualities. Husson remaps and reprioritizes physical sensibility in a way that raises questions about modernity and its hierarchy of the senses. The question remains whether she challenges norms in a way that merely emphasizes her own exclusion from them—her own difference—or whether there is something bold and resistant in her way of life.

Recently, scholars have seen connections between views of women and views of disabled people: both, for instance, are said to differ from "male" or "normal bodied" standards of what is good and valued. Husson's blindness and femininity unfolded in the oppressive conditions of nineteenth-century France. Since the early nineteenth century the Napoleonic Code stripped married women of their property (including their wages) and awarded it legally to their husbands, forced women to live where their husbands chose, prohibited them from serving as witnesses or having other rights and duties of citizenship, and withdrew from them legal control of their own children. Through this elimination of economic and civic independence, women were dependent, like—it could be argued—blind and other people with disabilities. As a result of their seclusion from the big world of money and power, women developed sensitivity and, like them, some disabled people were seen to be mild of temperament and attuned to others. However, Husson forces us to think about the relationship between femininity and disability and whether we might not equate these differences too easily. Her writings and her gripping life story clash with many of our expectations.

Without giving away any more of this book, I will say that Husson's "Reflections" and the course of her life

question our cultural stereotypes and our normal understanding of society. Disability studies has allowed us
almost miraculously to pose new questions about the
past, to probe our social hierarchies and values, and to
search out in authors like Husson the rich meanings of
embodiment.

BONNIE G. SMITH
Rutgers University

REFLECTIONS

I.

INTRODUCTION

CATHERINE J. KUDLICK AND
ZINA WEYGAND

When young Thérèse-Adèle Husson sat down to write her "Reflections" about being blind in 1825, she probably had no idea that she was committing a revolutionary act. Works by a blind person writing for the benefit of other blind people had rarely been published before. And if they had, they would surely have been written by men, as would be the case later in the century when a large number of them began to capture the public imagination in both France and America.[1] Before such writings had become widespread, the twenty-two-year-old woman from the small provincial city of Nancy set out on her own path. She hoped, as she stated in her opening paragraphs, to use her modest account to win the favor of Jean-Marie de La Croix d'Azolette, the director of the Quinze-Vingts Hospital, one of the only institutions in France open to support and lodge blind people in the first half of the nineteenth century. Founded by Saint Louis between 1254 and 1260, the ancient hospital had been established to serve three hundred—that is, quinze-vingts (fifteen times twenty)—poor blind people in Paris.

1

The Quinze-Vingts Hospital in 1866, drawing by Léon Gaucherel, in M. le Marquis de La Valette, *Les Etablissements généraux de bienfaisance placés sous le patronage de l'Impératrice* (Paris: Imprimerie Impériale, 1866).

Later it would admit indigent blind from the entire kingdom, also increasing the numbers of pensioners. Because of her plea, we have the extraordinary tale of a woman describing her life and ideas about everything from cloth to animals to marriage. More important, she did this in such a way that it opens up new possibilities for understanding women, disability, religion, and even—albeit unintentionally—a kind of nascent political consciousness in the generation after the French Revolution.

As Husson contemplated and wrote her "Reflections," France was trying to pull itself back together after nearly a generation of revolution and war. Beginning in 1789, a diverse coalition of intellectuals, peasants, merchants, and carpenters—to name the most obvious participants —had sought to reinvent a country no longer governed by a king, the nobility, and the Catholic Church. By the time the Revolution had reached its height, the Church had been abolished while the king and queen, along with numerous nobles who had not fled into exile, had been executed by the guillotine. The new rulers experimented with reinventing politics and culture itself based on the many exciting ideas circulating from Enlightenment thinkers at the end of the eighteenth century. Everything from one-man rule to asylums for people with disabilities to the calendar itself came into question. As the euphoric hopes from the early months dissolved into the realities of running a nation, the new France found itself beset not just by political strife but by economic difficulties and social unrest. War raged at home and abroad, making it a challenge to govern. A decade after the Revolution had begun, an authoritarian ruler came to power promising glory to the struggling nation. But not even the great Napoleon could remedy the situation, and because he had posed a threat to European stability, by 1814 France once again found itself ruled by the very Bourbon monarchy that had been defeated in 1789. Known as the Restoration, this constitutional monarchy brought back the Church and nobility that the years of revolution had banished. It also ushered in a new era of charitable paternalism toward blind people resulting from tight alliances between altar and crown. Born in 1803 under the rule of Napoleon, Thérèse-Adèle Husson came of age in a Restoration world that celebrated Old Regime values of piety, charity, and self-sacrifice. She would use these very ideas to win over representatives of the regime like La Croix d'Azolette.

But why would she even be interested in getting his attention? During the first half of the nineteenth century, blind people had very limited options in France, or anywhere else in the world, for that matter.[2] We don't even know exactly how many French people were blind, since no statistical data exist for the first half of the nineteenth century. Based on censuses that began counting blind people after 1850, we came up with the rough estimate of 35,000. But this figure is probably low, since no technical means existed to measure visual acuity or visual field at the time. In fact, definitions of blindness were based on qualitative criteria rather than quantitative measurements. Anyone who "does not see well enough to orient himself" and whose impairment rendered them "incapable of accomplishing the types of work requiring the sense of sight" provided a working definition of blindness that would remain in official use until 1945, when ophthalmologic criteria were introduced.[3] Not only did this make it difficult for blind people to be counted, but it also made it possible (and likely) that a significant number might not opt to identify themselves in this way.

Despite the complete absence of statistics, we can be certain that in nineteenth-century France, as in earlier times, most blind people came from the lower classes and faced extremely difficult lives. More often than not, their impairment kept or thrust them into misery. Blind people came disproportionately from among the poor both because the lower classes made up the majority of the French population in the early nineteenth century and because the major causes of blindness, such as illnesses, poor hygiene, malnutrition, and accidents on the job, were far more likely to accompany poverty.

Many factors might intervene to determine a blind person's fate. If someone had learned a trade while sighted, for example, they might find ways of practicing it after becoming blind later in life, whereas someone blind from an early age might never have been given the chance to learn at all. In addition, whether or not they enjoyed the support of family members also might play a role, since having help close at hand could be the key to survival if someone couldn't afford to hire servants to act as assistants or guides. The files of blind people who aspired for a space at the Quinze-Vingts tell us that the poorest remained quite isolated. Some were orphans, others were married and abandoned by their spouses, others were elderly people deserted by their children, and still others were widows and widowers whom political events and wars had deprived of their families' support. A number of these people lived in such misery and isolation that if they couldn't secure a place at the Quinze-

Vingts, they would stoop even lower to accept or even ask for a space in a general hospital, where blind individuals of all ages found themselves mixed in with the elderly, the incurably ill, and people with various other physical and mental disabilities.

Many blind people, even the poor, fared better than those who petitioned the Quinze-Vingts. When a family didn't suffer from complete destitution, it could afford the luxury of feeding what some at the time referred to as "a useless mouth." Such people performed minimal services in a household, and would one day survive on minimal assistance provided by local parish or municipal charity offices that supplied bread, vegetable soup, clothing, and sometimes cash handouts. Others worked as street singers or wandering musicians, for example, or animal trainers in traveling shows, wheel spinners, hawkers, sellers of pins or matches, fortune tellers, or distributors of lottery tickets. Far greater numbers simply begged, despite each successive government's attempts to prohibit the practice since the Revolution, and despite the occasional police sweeps to rid various cities of beggars throughout the Restoration.

Of course, not all blind people were poor and unknown. Thanks to testimonies written at the time, we know a good deal about a few privileged individuals, information that provides a more complex picture of blindness. Some were educated or managed to readjust to life without any help from an institution. Blind men, and an occasional woman, were scholars, musicians who performed in elite circles, mathematicians, and writers. The life of Chevalier Marie-Charles-Joseph de Pougens provides an example of how blind people might function in French society during Husson's time if they possessed adequate resources and drive.

Pougens lost his sight as an adult and managed to readjust to blindness by doing everything through secretaries who read to him and took dictation. Born in Paris in 1755, he was sent to Rome in 1776 to study diplomacy under the auspices of Cardinal Bernis. While there, at the age of twenty-three he contracted a severe case of smallpox that almost cost him his life, an experience he described in his *Mémoires et souvenirs*.[4] Blind in one eye and then both, due to two incompetent oculists, he later became a "grammarian" (known today as a linguist) and a translator. In 1795 he launched himself into a book-selling and printing business that included a literary journal started in 1800 called *Bibliothèque Française*, which survived for the next four years. Pougens was named a member of the Académie des Inscriptions et Belles Lettres in addition to several other erudite societies in France and abroad. Besides his masterpiece, *Treasure of Origins, or Reasoned Grammatical Dictionary of the French Language* (1819), he wrote several modestly successful novels, not to mention works of philology as well as small treatises on ethics and philosophy influenced by the spirit of the Enlightenment.[5] He was friends with the important *philosophe* d'Alembert and frequented publishing circles that attracted big names such as Barba and Panckoucke. Like all of the most respected European intellectuals of his day, he maintained literary correspondences with famous people in France and abroad, relying on his secretary, Théodore Lorin, whom he had hired in 1795 and who remained his faithful aide for thirty-eight years, "his friend and his son by adoption."[6] Contemporaries admired Pougens's erudition, affable temper, and tolerant views. Having retired to the small town of Vauxbuin, northeast of Paris, he died in 1833 surrounded by his wife and close friends. Pougens would leave a profound and positive impression on blind people in Husson's day by showing that one could live a fulfilling, even influential life as a married man.

It's difficult to determine Thérèse-Adèle Husson's social class based on her "Reflections." Knowing that she had written the manuscript in order to gain admission to the Quinze-Vingts might lead one to think that she came from a very modest, even poor background; after all, why else would she have gone to so much trouble to ingratiate herself to a man who ran one of the country's only refuges for blind people? Yet the language and ideas in the text reveal her to be much more educated than the average blind person coming from the lower classes; her choice of vocabulary and literary references suggest someone who had received a fine education not available to most people in France. This ambiguity makes it hard to pigeonhole the woman and her manuscript. It also invites us to look closely at everything in the "Reflections," from style to the choice of examples, for clues as to who Husson was.

We found the manuscript unobtrusively nestled in a folder at the archives of the Quinze-Vingts Hospital, to this day a major Parisian center for the treatment of eye diseases and disorders.[7] Not dated and seemingly unmarked by time, the medium-sized notebook consisted of eighty-three handwritten pages measuring approximately eight by six inches. We managed to determine a date by investigating the career of La Croix d'Azolette and placing it against certain facts from Husson's life and the history of the Quinze-Vingts. Since Louis Braille was only in the process of inventing his system of tactile reading through raised dots at the time Husson contemplated her "Reflections," her only way of setting them down would have been to ask someone—a relative, a professional scribe or secretary, a nun, a neighbor—to write for her. Judging from the handwriting and vastly different qualities of spelling and punctuation, we concluded that Husson dictated her manuscript to two people. We know nothing about either one, not even their gender (though, due to social conventions of the day, we strongly suspect that at least one was female). The only thing we can say with certainty is that one appeared to be much more literate than the other. The work's title and dedication, probably composed at the last minute, seemed to be very rough, so most likely these parts were transcribed on the spot—maybe even at the gates of the Quinze-Vingts —by someone with uncertain spelling skills. The body of the text, however, is drafted in a steady hand and contains few errors; a more educated person than the first probably proofread and carefully edited it.

Struck by Husson's rich descriptions, her candor, and her bravado, we engaged in long discussions about her possible background and what circumstances needed to have come together for her to have contemplated and written such a plea. Who was this remarkable young woman? To which social class did she belong? Where did she get the wherewithal to write her "Reflections"? Did they win over La Croix d'Azolette? And finally, what became of her?

Early pages from Husson's "Reflections," written by a scribe with uncertain spelling skills.

We embarked on a research detective odyssey to answer such questions after an amazing stroke of luck.
One afternoon, while leafing at random through the
title pages of nineteenth-century novels about blindness
collected at the Association Valentin Haüy Library in
Paris, we found a novel by a woman named "Madame
Foucault" with the tiny printed notation "born Adèle
Husson, blind woman from Nancy" beneath it. Some
hasty cross-checking at various libraries and publishing
houses in Paris revealed that before she died at the age of
twenty-eight, our Adèle had in fact gone on to publish
ten novels after writing her "Reflections," which she
never did publish, even though this was perhaps her
boldest and most original writing. Months of archival
work followed. Eventually, we managed to reconstruct
the intriguing life and untimely death of a blind woman
from the provinces who sought to make her way alone in
the bustling French capital.

In the process of piecing together Husson's life, we
stumbled on another bit of good fortune: the preface to
one of Madame Foucault's early books, *Story of a Pious
Heiress* (1828), contained further details about her life.[8]
We decided to include it in this volume immediately after
her "Reflections" in order to give readers a fuller picture
in her own words. Such a preface (like the mention of the
author's blindness on the title pages from some of her
books) aimed no doubt to win public sympathy and interest regarding the writer's unique perspective. But
when read after her more moralistic "Reflections" and
then in the context of the life we discovered through
other sources, Husson emerges as a character filled with
ambiguities, surprises, and stunning contradictions. Her

need to present herself one way while living quite another reveals how she struggled to fashion an identity in the face of many competing personal and social influences.

Defying easy categorization, this young writer raises a number of questions at the heart of issues both past and present. Was she a feminist? What was the relationship between her being a woman and being blind? What new perspective can this one woman's disability bring to our understanding of class and gender? And how did class and gender in turn shape her options as a blind person in the 1820s? However we contemplate these questions and the rich variety of possible answers, we must keep in mind that Husson wrote these texts over 175 years ago, when the ideas of women's rights and class difference had only just been introduced by the French Revolution.

What follow, then, are Husson's "Reflections" and the preface to her *Story of a Pious Heiress*, "Notes on the Author's Youth," both published in their entirety. After our readers have had a chance to meet her and form their own impressions, we conclude this volume with a more detailed discussion of her life, her world, and the broader implications for how we might think about history, literature, and society. While we have done much archival work in order to tell her story, we leave the texts themselves open for readers to discover and interpret on their own. Her discussion of the senses, for example, offers much food for thought that transcends time and place.

Before we launch into Husson's writings, a few preliminary comments must be made. We have tried to respect the style and punctuation of the originals, adding to them only when this was the only way of making her meaning clear. Occasionally we have added brief explanations in square brackets, or have included Husson's original wording in French where there may be a question about our English translation. Readers of the twenty-first century may at first find parts confusing and the style a bit cloying, particularly the manner in which Husson felt she needed to prostrate herself in order to convince the fervent Catholics who ran the Quinze-Vingts that she deserved their protection. Even so, Husson expressed strong opinions, not all of them necessarily held by the people she hoped to impress or even by other blind people. Her texts must be taken on their own terms, written as they were in the style of her day. At the same time, she speaks to many things that people with disabilities still debate even today.

Finally, we'd like to offer a few words of thanks. We acknowledge the administration of the Quinze-Vingts for granting us permission to publish the "Reflections." Thérèse de Raedt and Louise-Hélène Trouilloud helped with translation. The Western Society for French History continued its tradition of nurturing scholarship that is new and different by accepting a panel devoted entirely to a person no one had ever heard of before; Stanford University's French Cultural Studies group provided a forum for a lively discussion of the "Reflections." Meanwhile, many people in France and the United States helped by offering information and advice, reading the manuscript, and urging us onward. Among them, we want especially to thank Philippe Boutry, Anthony Candela, Marianne Constable, Alain Corbin (who introduced us), Georgina Kleege, Sheryl Kroen, Evelyne

Lejeune-Resnick, JoBurr Margadant, Barbara Pierce, and Madame Renson, archivist for the city of Nancy. Bonnie G. Smith deserves special mention because of her intellectual generosity and encouragement, and for flying six thousand miles in less than twenty-four hours simply so she could participate in a ninety-minute discussion of our work-in-progress. Thanks also to Professor Kudlick's students and colleagues at the University of California, Davis, for providing their first impressions of Husson and her "Reflections." Finally, we are grateful to Niko Pfund, formerly of New York University Press, who believed in this project from the start and made it happen, and to the History of Disability Series general editors, Paul Longmore and Lauri Umansky, and Eric Zinner, Rosalie Morales Kearns, and the staff at NYU Press who saw it through to its conclusion.

II.

Reflections on the Physical and Moral Condition of the Blind

ADÈLE HUSSON

Translated from the French by Catherine J. Kudlick

Physical and Moral Condition of the Blind, dedicated to Monsieur La Croix d'Azolette, Director General of the Royal Hospice of the Quinze-Vingts, Squire and Knight [Ecuryer et Chevalier] of Saint Louis, holder of the Legion of Honor, Cavalry Captain with authorization

Sir, before obtaining from you the honorable favor of offering you the homage of this mediocre production, I dared not let it see the light of day. But your touching kindness has encouraged me, and permits me to hope for your indulgence, of which I have the greatest need. If in the course of this work you notice an incorrect style, the principles of morality and religion that lie at its base, along with my young age, will surely win your pardon. My misfortune is the strong desire that I be pleasing to you, as well as to my unfortunate comrades. If I speak more directly to women in a state of blindness, it is because their situation inspires in me an interest that is as strong as it is tender. Might you, kind sir, share and grant me an approving smile in reading a person whose goal is to always please you and merit your esteem.

I have the honor, with respect, sir, of being your most humble and obedient servant.

T. A. Husson

Foreword

One looks upon the use of sight as one of the greatest fortunes. I cannot share this opinion. I was deprived of my sight at the age of nine months. I have just reached my twenty-second year, and I still don't remember ever having formed a single regret concerning the loss of my eyes, a loss that seems to me to be of little importance, because people who see tell me, "You don't have the slightest understanding of treasures you have never known." I would like to believe in the justice of this reasoning, which, however, does nothing to persuade me that I am unhappy; if anything, it's the sad exclamations of people who see me that do that. But I am far from being so callous as to resist these demonstrations of compassion; they evoke in me an extreme gratitude, even if at times they cause me great sorrow. People who console me hope to better my lot, but alas! they only make it worse. I have waited a long time [for an article that needs to be developed on this subject]. By bringing forth this feeble product, I do not merely intend to make the public familiar with my feelings, my character, and my ideas. I shall also attempt to paint a picture of my comrades of misfortune, such as they are and such as they should be. Here follows what makes my misfortune easy for me.

A girlfriend who was very dear to me, and whom an untimely death carried away from me as well as from her adoring parents, also had to endure the loss of sight. The similarity of our situation, along with that of our tastes and characters, established a boundless affection and trust between us. We kept not a single secret from one another; I responded to all her questions with the same frankness with which she replied to mine. Never could envy or discord have had the power to alter our tender friendship. Always united in heart and mind, the intimate union that made us each so happy charmed our parents. My friend's step and demeanor [*maintien*] often caused our acquaintances to mistake her for me, something that shouldn't surprise anyone who has seen blind people; they can't ignore the fact that there exists a certain resemblance among everyone stricken with blindness. I will hasten to explain my reasoning. Returning to my kind companion and me, I would say that our touch had the same keenness, we received an identical education, and our mutual attachment increased the cheerfulness that nature provided us with even more. We were so accustomed to our lot that when one day I asked my friend what she desired most in the world, she responded, putting her arms around me, "The happiness of everyone I love." When I continued, "But Charlotte, you could wish first for your own happiness," she answered in a tender tone, "It's your affection that I always want to have, but the return of my sight, would it not bring our happiness to its peak? On the contrary, I would fear that the return of my sight would destroy our friendship because we would have less in common." "Oh, good Charlotte," I cried with enthusiasm, "if God willed me to see again, I would beg Him to leave me in physical darkness, which I cherish so much because I share it with you."

I've given this brief account in the hopes that it will show my readers the full extent of the keenness of our friendship. We did not seek to hide our surprise when people deigned to praise our resignation. May the blind people who are distraught by their destiny be pitied! Charlotte said, "They always have an air of sadness about them. The profound distress on their faces can only inspire pity; but only kindness and solid virtues have by themselves the power to inspire the interest of other people." I agreed with my companion, for from her mouth always came wisdom and reason. We each learned with equal facility everything that we were taught. Our good and indulgent schoolmistresses treated us with truly maternal tenderness; never scolded, always filled with consideration and ready to give a caressing hand, in every sense the recipients of continual benevolence, we constantly repeated to one another that those who see couldn't possibly enjoy such bliss as ours. Alas! The cruel Fates only let us enjoy our happiness for a short time. Oh Divine Providence! I do not murmur against your inscrutable decrees. Imitating my beloved Charlotte, I want to die in adoring your invaluable decrees, and you, angelic creature, you who were so long my friend, if from the height of Heaven where your virtues have no doubt placed you, if you deign to remember your childhood companion, intercede in her favor, and obtain from the merciful God the force and the grace to accomplish the task that pity has imposed on her, the strong wish to be of use and pleasing to all blind people.

But let me return to my subject, from which the memory of a cherished friend distracted me for an instant; if a frank and close friendship existed between two people stricken with blindness, why would others, similarly deprived of sight, and gifted with a sound judgment and a strong devotion, not be pleased to imitate them? Yes, just and noble God! You will allow these sensitive beings to console one another, teach each other to be mutually patient; this hope electrifies me, it is this that has the exclusive power to ease a part of the difficulties presented by the work I am about to undertake. It will seem easy to me if, in reducing the hardships of my comrades of misfortune, I can manage to prove to them that in supporting them religiously, they only accomplish the will of the sovereign arbiter of the universe.

In speaking to my readers of the dear companion that I lost, my intention is to show that if I make certain generalizations about the physical and moral condition of blind people, my relationship with another person deprived of sight gives me in some ways the right. In addition, I've always taken a certain pleasure in seeking out the company of other blind people, and when I ask them about their feelings, characters, and ideas, their responses enable me to establish a comparison between me and them. It is not without profound reflection and without being deeply immersed in my topic that I decided to begin this work, and if my readers attach a certain price to this unwavering devotion to my subject, I dare to hope that they will grant me their indulgence, keeping in mind that darkness engulfs me always, and that I live, think, and act only from tradition.

CHAPTER 1

On the Gait and Demeanor of the Blind

I shall first speak of how we walk, which is considered trembling and uncertain. Forgive me, dear reader, if I dare to say frankly that this is less our fault than it is that of those who surround us. When a very young blind child makes a few steps on his own, his parents or his friends hasten to tell him in a tone easily recognized as horror, "Be careful, you will hurt yourself; if I were you I wouldn't dare take such risks!" These warnings, which come from people with only the most loving of intentions, inspire in us suspicion, even terror that is impossible to overcome. The people charged with looking after us would render an important service by protecting us at an early age against such fears that so often are only imaginary. I anticipate the response of my readers, who are convinced that blind people should always remain in a state of complete immobility. Watching the blind walking or doing things will naturally lead those who watch over us with affectionate interest to assume that we are in danger, but this exists only in their imagination. One couldn't be more useful to us than by accustoming us from childhood on to walk without a guide, and by building up our courage with kind and reassuring words from the earliest age. In my family no one ever stopped repeating over and over, "Don't be afraid of anything, I'm watching over you." So I placed all my confidence in this promise, and I played happily with girls my own age.

Since I've promised to speak sincerely, I should also add that a certain degree of coquettishness also enters into how we carry ourselves, and here I speak only of female companions of misfortune. When we are confident enough to be clothed in a pretty dress and dainty shoes, decked out in these luxurious things, which mean as much to us as they do to people who see, we wouldn't want to sit or stand the way we are used to and the way we think we should because we're so worried about how we might look. For us it seems like the slightest movement will alter the beauty of our clothes. This fear gives us the appearance of being extremely self-conscious, a terrible embarrassment spreads over us, the source of which remains a mystery for those who look at us; instead they attribute our awkwardness to the griefs brought by our afflicted situation. We thus inspire tender emotions as people console us, feel sorry for us, when in fact they should be punishing our pride. It's surely because of the pretty dress and pretty shoes that we don't even dare to take a step, even being guided. Our guide will not even notice the elegance of our finery, which water and pebbles will surely ruin. This fear increases our mistrust, and it's only with difficulty that we put one foot in front of the other. Our apprehensions gradually slow down our gait and make it uneven, which has always led me to believe that we must tire the person who offers us the help of his arm. I was never allowed to forget that we carry ourselves rigidly. Nothing could be further from the truth, but if we lean backwards, it's easy to imagine, given how suspicious and fearful we are naturally, how much we dread bumping into objects in our way. I also know that people reproach us for tilting our heads upwards, but I will respond that this position comes from the rigidity of how we carry ourselves. I've thought seriously about how I could eliminate these faults, which result from deeply ingrained habits. All my efforts have been fruitless, and I no longer flatter myself with the hope of seeing them crowned with success.

CHAPTER 2

On the Touch of the Blind

Everyone lauds the extreme finesse of the sense of touch among people stricken with blindness, in fact you'd think that some even envy it. But were it in their power to give up this precious advantage that they have because of the generosity of the King of Kings, they would not want to relinquish it, even for the price of a crown. It seems that the Divine Creator of all things, in plunging a certain number of His children into physical darkness, accords them a moral clarity that shines in their smallest actions. From these celestial rays emanating from their souls is born the exquisite sense of touch that inspires so much surprise and admiration in those who see. It would be difficult, even impossible, to trick blind people by making them touch certain objects while giving the wrong names. Permit me to give an example on this subject. I had just turned eleven when my parents ordered me to prepare myself for one of the most venerable and imposing moments in life; in a few months I was to take my First Communion. For the day following this beautiful event, my mother had promised me a chiffon dress, but she contented herself with buying me one made of percale instead, which she offered to me, saying, "This is splendid chiffon." After touching the material, I responded, "This is very pretty percale." She assured me that I was wrong, but I refused to believe her. That afternoon, several ladies came over to our house, and since she had begged them to join with her in persuading me that the dress she had bought me was made of chiffon, they went along with her story. But I interrupted them, saying, "Dear ladies, do you believe what you are telling me?" All responded affirmatively. "In that case," I continued, without being disconcerted, "I prefer my touch to your eyes, because it allows me to appreciate things for what they really are, whereas it seems to me that your sight fools you now and then, for this is percale and not chiffon." This exchange amused my mother as well as the ladies, and in the end I received the dress that she promised. The blind can distinguish equally well between materials that have a certain resemblance, such as taffeta, real and fake merino. There are even some who are capable of telling whether a book is printed in large or small characters simply by touching it. Their delicate touch serves them marvelously when they want to learn music. Almost all people deprived of sight know the people who are dear to them through touch; they have no greater happiness than being near to the objects of their affection. When they hear them and touch them the pure joy that animates them would lead one to think that they don't regret anything in this world. Oh! If it's true that the eyes contribute to the human's bliss, only touch, hearing, and speech have the power to assure it. May the gratefulness of the blind be toward the Supreme Being for the benefits with which He fills them each day, they possess the faculty of smell united with that of hearing and the ability to express themselves; and this perfect sense of touch? Is it not to you, my God, that we owe this vital sense? Sovereign arbiter of their fate, do they not have the right to be moved by it? Could the loss of such a useful and agreeable sense inspire a glimmer of regret in their hearts when your liberal hand spreads your precious favors over them? No, powerful God, the blind will never grumble against your sublime decrees; their only glory will be to adore God's decrees throughout their lives, and they will be happy to submit themselves religiously to your holy will. The love and confidence that they have in you, along with a lively, solid faith, and by the sweet hope of seeing their Divine Master in the next world, and to be among His select few. . . . Oh, consoling devotion! Support the courage of all people in a state of blindness, inspire in them the necessary resignation to obtain an eternal life, the object of all their sighs and all their wishes, and touch! You! Delicious touch that excites in the soul of the blind a religious enthusiasm: receive also from these sensitive beings for whom you sweeten misfortune this tribute of praise that they owe you for these always new, inexhaustible joys that you bring them.

CHAPTER 3

The Distinctive Character of the Blind

Fearful, defiant, sweet but impassioned, these are more or less the faults and the qualities that characterize the blind. It is as easy to explain the motives as it is to conceive of them. Fear is natural for these unfortunates because everyone who notices them seems to bring it to their attention. When they appear in public the stares of the multitude are fixed upon them, and agonizing words strike their ears: "What a shame!" "How unfortunate!" "Death would be preferable to such a cruel privation!" There are even some people who seek out the blind to tell them these things so they don't miss any of the sad exclamations. This sad pity does not merit being confused with benevolent interest, because this noble sentiment has no other language than that which comes from the heart. It is through his actions that we can best admire the person. Those blind from birth do not know what light is, and would not even miss it without the indiscreet phrases too often uttered in their presence. We have good reason to be pitied, people stricken with blindness tell themselves, because in virtually every situation our lot gives rise to such painful compassion. They are never distracted, and if by misplaced zeal their friends paint to them a delightful picture of all that they admire, the blind who are pious [and] who are resigned, feel neither pain nor regrets [. . .] but it seems to them that the intelligence that God has granted them is infinitely superior to this physical light that they constantly hear being talked about. This idea electrifies them, it excites their hearts and raises their souls almost to the height of the heavenly beings. Not being able to appreciate anything on this earth of exile, they all yearn for the final happy moment that must unite them with their Divine Master. The superficial and unimportant objects can win their affections, which are maybe as extreme as their suspicion and their fear. The blind love with excess because, as I have just said, their attachment is not obstructed by anything banal. A pleasing face, gracious manners, and a few talents, these are priceless treasures for those who see. If by some misfortune, a likable person is disgraced by nature, she only inspires a sterile and sometimes disdainful pity. The blind, who because of their position must be less superficial, usually show better judgment. Virtue produces on them the same effect as beauty does for people who see, with this one difference: the feelings of one group, founded on a solid moral base, are much more long-lasting than those of the other. External charms fade rapidly, but such is not the case for those that adorn the soul. Ugliness follows attractiveness, but goodness, beauty, sweetness united with piety, spirit, reason survive as long as the one who hears them. But what do I say? They will live on. All the reflections of the blind on this subject are moral and dictated by a pious enthusiasm, to which they give themselves over without restraint. However, their exaltation sometimes has a less noble, less laudable motive, often its origins lie in the readings imposed on the blind without their choice or judgment.

CHAPTER 4

The Previous Subject Continued

As with misfortune, sensitivity is not shared by all humans, [and] there are some who severely blame people deprived of sight [for their own situation]. Lacking in indulgence, these cold beings without pity for the lot of the unfortunate who has a right to be taken care of by the general interest [*ont droit à l'intérêt général*], they regularly call the elation of the blind a ridiculous and fabulous extravagance. This last epithet might work for some of those who have lost their sight, but can one justly blame them for unreasonable enthusiasm if reading novels has in effect distorted their judgment? Isn't this more the fault of the people around them than their own? The blind are also reproached for forming attachments too easily; in forming numerous links of friendship, both men and women afflicted with blindness will not be blamed by those beings who form a correct idea of their situation. For not being able to do anything without the help of the sighted, they use everything to capture their attention, and if they have gotten it, then their attachment is boundless, but when the person of their affections leaves them, one must forgive them for the speed with which they seek a new friend. The absent one always keeps a firm hold over their hearts; however, the one who replaces him quickly becomes both dear and indispensable. The explanation for our conduct is easy to give: being the never ending object of the care and attention of those who see, the blind all have enough good sense to notice that it is fortunate that one can provide what they need.

When they are sure that they are being helped through motives of good grace, they will pay this back most tenderly, and will stop at nothing to please this person. They jettison all sad ideas from their memories, and in the hope of pleasing their friend, they show themselves to be lighthearted. People admire their gaiety, are even surprised by it, and one would never even consider that this was a natural consequence [of blindness]. Sweetness and patience are two qualities that belong by nature to the blind. They are sweet in character, and one might even say that they are this way out of self-interest. As an ancient writer noted judiciously, one can do good without seeing but eyes are indispensable for doing evil. Thus a person stricken with blindness can and must be good. If she possesses the kernel of sensitivity, it is extremely easy for her to acquire this angelic sweetness that charms those she meets. Another reason leads the blind to endure without complaint the changing moods of those who govern them; how could they escape a dependence that must last their whole lives? Such is probably a question that she must ask herself, and incapable of responding in a satisfactory manner, these unfortunates take the wisest and most reasonable path. Willingly they submit themselves to the wills of others, and they rarely show the slightest trace of sorrow. Their patience and their admirable sweetness that distinguish them are truly necessary; when they dread something, it is because of the aid of these two precious advantages that the blind embellish their memory, and familiarize themselves with manual labor. Elation is a feeling that animates beings deprived of sight. In order to reach an understanding of the motives of this elation, one needs briefly to establish a comparison between the blind and the sighted; the latter admire everything that catches their eye. Thousands of diverse and charming objects capture their attention; the majesty of the sky, the beauty of the sun, the brightness of the stars, the pale yet magnificent light of the moon, all these masterpieces created by the arbiter of their lot excite within the soul of those who see a thousand delicious sensations. The blind do not have the power to contemplate the attractiveness of nature, but they rejoice in the capacity to smell. Their soul can receive the most vivid and most profound impressions.

CHAPTER 5

On the Inflection of a Sweet Voice on the Heart and Senses of a Blind Person

Now we come to a very important point; I would prefer that it was still possible for me not to take it up, but since this is the place to discuss it, and since I would not want anyone to reproach me for deliberately omitting it, I submit myself with good grace to speak of the impression produced by a sweet voice on our hearts and our senses; is there nothing in the world, I appeal to my girlfriends, that excites in our souls a comparable rapture to that caused by the flattering and benevolent accents that always come from a sensitive and tender heart; harmonious sounds electrify and entirely captivate our trust. Without reserve, we give ourselves over to the affection inspired by the one in whom we've heard a sweet voice; we are almost persuaded that a being who possesses such a

29

precious advantage has no faults. It would be difficult to change our minds. I think that agreeable sounds must also please those who see. As for us, we have no greater happiness than to enjoy the company of those whose voices charm us, [oh] touching organ! Gift from Heaven, you are also entitled to our gratitude. You help us endure our hardship. But what do I say, we have none, for your generous accents put an end to our unhappiness, and eliminate it down to the smallest trace. You have the power to embellish our existence and to light up our hearts, which can only be deliciously stirred by your inestimable treasures. I am most certain that my male and female companions who do not have the advantage of possessing such a beautiful voice, envy the lot of mortals, from whom according to us you are the most noble embellishment. How many people would be guilty of linking an enchanting voice with the horrible art of secretiveness that eclipsed the esteem and friendship of those with whom they had once enjoyed harmonious relations? In betraying them, these people can condemn us to eternal regrets, because if this misfortune would befall those of us deprived of sight, nothing would equal the violence of our despair. Extreme in everything, we would painfully say to ourselves, oh my God, who can then be trusted? How painful it would be to think that no more virtue exists on earth! May Heaven never allow such sad reflections to be ours! Let us hope that we will never be allowed to be deceived by the monsters of hypocrisy that profit from the sublime advantage that I praise, making a game, a mockery out of the candid innocence and the most sacred virtues; we would like to believe that those who possess a charming voice are gifted with an even more ravishing soul. When we hear them, a fire with nothing human about it courses through our veins and fills our faces, our mouth is half open and our tongue tied; we don't form a single word, but how expressive our silence truly is! Sometimes it is interpreted as it should be, but more often it is taken for being idiotic; however, the longest phrases are not the ones that are the most pleasing. On the contrary, I believe that long phrases must be bothersome. A single word pronounced in an affectionate, moving tone, very well-chosen expressions could never be more charming. I don't know if the inflections of a sweet voice create as much pleasure for men deprived of sight as they do for women afflicted with the same misfortune; we are always infinitely sensitive to the interest the people of our own sex are willing to take in us.

But surely we will probably be pardoned for feeling an even more lively satisfaction in hearing those of the opposite sex. Where does this marked preference come from? We do not know, but it exists [and] it is impossible to hide; when a man comes up to us, we recognize him even without his having spoken or touched us; does he make himself heard? If his voice offers a delicious harmony, nothing equals our happiness. We answer his questions with a distracted and embarrassed air; our blush, for the man has learned that the fire that livens our faces is the color red, and as a result I say that our blush is sufficient evidence for those who speak with us of the sweet emotion that preys upon us. People who want easily to find the way to our hearts will have the goodness to speak to us in an extremely sweet tone, and [this will] always make us infinitely grateful to them.

CHAPTER 6

The Joys That Hearing Brings to the Blind

When I started this work by saying that blindness offered an incalculable number of charms, I was not deceiving my readers, who must have already noticed them, for I seek to prove to my readers that far from imposing on them, I have only dimly painted the advantages that we enjoy, I first spoke to them of those joys brought by touch.

Now I am going to introduce them to the joys brought to us by hearing, and I am persuaded that after having listened to me, they will no longer dare to permit themselves to bombard us with that cold and disdainful pity that offends us so much. It is to our ears that we owe the pleasure of being able to judge the sound of a voice more or less affectionate. Thanks to our hearing, music is also a priceless treasure for us; a sweet harmony produced by no matter what instrument soothes our souls with a consoling and invigorating balm that suspends all our powers without ruining them; let no one tell me now that a deaf person is happier than we blind people [because] an overture, a sonata, a duo, a love song haven't the slightest charm for this unfortunate. But for us! What a difference! To appreciate the lyre of Orpheus and the charming art of Apollo the muses cannot declare war on us as they did with the deaf and mute, for we have the satisfaction of judging their qualities, and sometimes we even celebrate them. If we go to a performance we can freely give our opinion on the tone and voices of the actors, we remember the interesting passages of the plays that have just been performed as well as the couplets if there are any. We take pleasure in conversations [and] respond as best we can to the questions the people around us enjoy asking. We often hear it said that we are interesting; finally, we receive flattering compliments that couldn't be given to people deprived of hearing and speech. I am certain that if one wanted to make the effort to question them through the use of signs, they would say that our situation is preferable to theirs, for if we are taken to church a preacher with a gracious voice is always sure to win our approval. Instead, the deaf and mute gives the impression at a performance, a concert, and even in the midst of well-chosen company, as well as at church, of being inept. And this even if he is blessed with beautiful and good eyes. So, go ahead, envy their lot, you who pity ours. Do we find ourselves in gatherings? We mingle in conversations without effort, regardless of the direction it takes. If a witticism escapes from one of the members of the group, our faces light up and we laugh with the same heartiness as those who see. However, deaf and mute people are always embarrassed, distrustful, restrained when they find themselves in the midst of a gathering; being unable to hear what is being said around them, they are surely convinced that their unhappiness is the exclusive topic of conversation; incapable of participating, they are constantly sad; dreamers and carefully seeking solitude, they can't make friends like we can, only understanding with difficulty and being understood with equal difficulty. These people can't know if they have a heart, for unlike ours, that of the deaf-mute is not animated with a thousand delicious sensations; being unable to judge feelings, they can feel neither sympathy nor friendship. I am aware that several of them must possess rare and pleasing knowledge [*sciences*], but these advantages for which I sincerely congratulate them don't even come close to those brought to us by the sense of which they are deprived and by which we too can acquire talents. It seems to me that it requires less hard work for me, and that we give our teachers less trouble than the unfortunates whose situation can cause just reason for complaint. We know how to cherish because we can hear; we like conversation because it is possible to participate in it; we like being interviewed because we know we respond easily. We have no trouble conceiving that deaf and mutes don't have as many advantages, are infinitely more unhappy than we are; this is why each day we must thank the Supreme Being for the graces that He has deigned to give us, let us not forget, above all, that in muttering against our destiny we are offending this Divine Providence from which we must respect the smallest decrees.

CHAPTER 7

*Ideas That Blind People Form Concerning the
Sun and the Moon*

I'm going to stop speaking to my readers about that which concerns our habits in order to give them an idea of how we judge things. I will teach them what ideas we form of the heavens and the sun. Because these objects can be seen but not touched, it is impossible that the way we envision them is always the most correct. According to the questions we customarily ask, it seems to us that the sky might be compared with a veil of the finest cloth, such as tulle or gauze. Say if you like that it is blue, as those of us who have never seen only know this color by name. We should be forgiven if we do not pass judgment, for our situation makes this impossible. Thus, as I have just said, according to us the sky is a veil. We compare it to this object of luxury as much because we intend to celebrate its beauty as because in our readings one speaks constantly to us of its admirable light; because we were also told that it was sprinkled with brilliant stars, my friend and I had the habit of touching sequins, which we considered to be stars, despite the fact that we were told several times that stars were much larger. Thus the sky, I repeat for the third time, is a veil sown with sequins that run through the entire universe, because its expanse is immense; but when the weather clouds over we are convinced, to use the phrase of people who see, that the stars disappear, that they are replaced by spots similar to those that we can make on our clothes with ink or coal, having heard that these two objects were black, and that the color that tarnishes the beautiful veil is also the same, we link the one with the other; such is our reasoning with regard to the sky. I have no doubt that my readers find it extremely narrow-minded, but it is impossible for us to have any other idea because our touch can't be useful. This, I confess, is unfortunate, but we can console ourselves by dreaming that if we don't see the ravishing exterior of the heavens in this world, God will deign to permit us to see its perfect interior in the next. This hope should make all our disappointments bearable.

As for the sun, approximately here is how we see it;

35

because the world is round, as geography teaches us, the sun that entirely heats it all must also be round as it beams down on us. We are not surprised to hear people who see assert that they can't look straight at it; when it warms us we find it appealing, but if it inconveniences us, it immediately loses its attractions. Therefore, we judge it according to the sensations it brings us; its color is foreign to us because we know only the name of these prerogatives of every object, and we don't know if they have more or less value [unless] someone has the kindness to instruct us about it. I'll therefore stick with saying that our imagination presents the sun as a round ball, one that is extremely blazing; we thank and admire its Creator who is also our own; we were taught that He only allowed this star to shine in order to increase the survival of all human beings who have to adore God as much as we do, and who are eternally grateful to Him for the constant signs of the tender and eternal concern they receive.

CHAPTER 8

On Men, Women, and Animals

In this work I will not offer a chapter about colors because this item, which we can't judge, should barely occupy a few lines. I will therefore content myself by saying so as not to return to this subject, that blue, white, green, pink leave us indifferent to their many charms since we don't know them better. If we dare to describe them, it would surely not be our ideas that we would bring to light, but simply those of people who see. I leave these visible objects in order to discuss palpable ones. I want to talk about men and women, which to me seems not very hard to do; our ideas can be quite correct regarding men and women, given the fact that we who are deprived of sight of either sex can envision those who are members of our own sex, for the bodies of those who see are absolutely the same as ours. Moreover, we don't exist without touching people who approach us, which makes the comparison that we establish between them and us quite easy. As for the expression of their physiognomy, the idea that we form of it always comes from the impression that the sound of their voice makes upon our hearts; if it is pleasant, we judge the face to be extremely sweet; if on the contrary it is harsh, we think that the exterior must be that way too. We make a mistake concerning one of these two suppositions only rarely, which makes people who listen to us say that we are infinitely shrewd, but in this, as in many other things, only our ear merits being praised. Women stricken with blindness judge men who want to be solicitous of them. They are convinced that such men must be blessed with an interesting face and a sensitive heart. But I warn these gentlemen that we are very hard on the tone and the manners of those with whom we converse; above all, we desire that they not be lacking in spirit; but we would gladly forgive them this misfortune if at least they possessed healthy judgment. I am most certain that blind men think in the same manner regarding the members of our sex; however, although I said in the sixth chapter of this work that we didn't attach any price to frivolous trivialities as those who see do, and which they tend to refer to as charms. I don't know if we are led by curiosity or by another feeling for which I could not and do not want to give a name, but when we love someone, and this cherished person goes away from us, our inferiors or our equals are overwhelmed by questions on his account; we want to know if he is big and well-built because we are able to say what constitutes a big, well-built person, for several among us have these advantages, which I believe aren't bad. We rarely inquire about faces, because, as I have already said, the sound of the voice directs our judgment.

As for animals, since we can touch different ones we appreciate them more or less according to whether they please us or not. For example, the dog. This good animal that we look upon as the loyal protector of men and who shows a constant interest in people who do not see, is in particular the object of our benevolent affection. He receives our caresses and we give them with the sweetest recognition. We believe ourselves to be invincible with this precious guardian at our sides. I won't dwell long on the sensation in us caused by cats; my friend and I had an insurmountable aversion to these animals. I can't say for certain if all blind people share these feelings, [but] having been clawed by them, we feared cats more than anything in the world. When we heard them, we made our fears so obvious that our relatives and friends could only dissipate them by chasing away the creatures that were the cause. The cry of these animals has something ferocious about it; when it reached our ears from far away our terror returned and our aversion took on even greater force. Pigeons, birds always inspire in us a sweet feeling just like they are; we touch them with pleasure. Horses scare us a bit because of how fast they run. In my Educational Plan I will tell what means our parents and teachers must use to familiarize us with every kind of animal. I have not yet spoken of sheep because their goodness is too well known for them to give rise to a mistrustful fear in us. Since livestock aren't the least bit appealing and only exist for our use, I have always moved away from them with care; I only have a very obscure idea of them, which, moreover, is not complimentary, and thus my readers will not be surprised if I refrain from talking about them.

CHAPTER 9

About My Ideas on Flowers, Furniture, and Cloth

Flowers, furniture, and cloth also have a place in this work; readers probably wouldn't mind knowing what ideas we form regarding these objects of which I will speak about more easily [because] all three serve to please or are useful to us. I shall begin by praising flowers whose delicious smell infinitely flatters us. We like them very much, but since we know that they wither, we never touch them without the greatest care; we imagine them as being very beautiful. But my judicious readers say to me, do you know what it means to be beautiful? Certainly I will answer them, considering this question to be important. It is to charm the eyes of people who see, as a work, a piece of verse, or a piece of music is charming to our ear; we had the habit of designating that which pleases us, saying, "How beautiful that is! How ravishing!" People who see speak like this. If our ideas make us find flowers appealing, they do so because there is a direct link between the ideas we have created of them and what they really are. Brilliant rose, whose odor creates an agreeable sensation, you always offer me the image of a pure soul, and if you were not to fade, I would believe that in holding you I would be enjoying a true friend. Sweet carnation, translator of a good heart! I determine no difference between you and the rose except for that necessitated by the shape and smell, for both of you offer me a divine charm; your beauty for me contains the same perfection. Little violet! Your flexibility diminishes nothing of the pleasures that you bring to our organs; you are so sweet that if you were more consistent, I would be surprised not to hear close to you the cooing of turtledoves both young and old; our imagination lends you almost as many advantages as the rose and the carnation. I also celebrate the pleasures of jasmine, of the reseda, the pansy; nor do I forget the lily of the valley; noble jasmine you flatter our taste just like your two friends with whom I compare you; in charming us, you are sure to please us. In so far as you are concerned, our ideas about you are the same, if I make an exception for the difference in shapes produced by the flowers of which I have just spoken; that is to say that every one that has a sweet odor introduces a feeling into our souls that resembles them. But someone will say that what you tell me on the subject of these flowers seems more appropriate as a defense of flowers than as an explanation of your ideas. I would respond without getting upset that our ideas are our feelings, or that at least they are directed by them, and because our tastes owe their existence to them, it seems to me that in tracing our feelings I am tracing our thoughts as well. Let us move on to furniture. Since there are some pieces that are absolutely necessary, when we are allowed to use them our touch serves as our eyes, and helps us in examining them with care. We know full well that a chest of drawers is square, but more long than tall. Again I hear my readers ask what is a square object! I am accommodating enough to satisfy all their questions. Therefore, I would say to them that it is easy enough to know the difference between objects by touching them, for not all of them have the same shape. For example, a dinner plate, a dish, a glass can't begin to be compared with a chest of drawers, for the first two are round, while the other is hollow; but people will probably point out that it is only after having heard the names of the articles that I designate that it became possible for me to acquire the certainty that they were hollow, round, square. I will admit that they are right, but tell me, you with the eyes of Argus, if you had never heard objects described, would you be in any better position to speak of them than I? Except by substituting other names and other qualities than their own? Frankness obliges you to respond in the negative; we appreciate and judge all furniture more or less according to utility and appeal.

Cloth is of a strict necessity because we need it in order to clothe ourselves, but those of luxury, what I take to be the most brilliant, such as satin, levantine, taffeta, muslin, percale, merino, and fine Indian fabrics, always capture our imagination, and obtain a marked preference over frieze, and fabrics that are more or less rough that are used for linens. It's the softness and fineness of cloth that we appreciate. Our touch, as I said in the chapter that took up this sense, is a great aid to us, providing us

41

with the means for forming quite correct ideas on every touchable object, ideas that are easier to conceptualize than to describe. Upon careful reflection regarding our manner of thinking with respect to our clothing, I cannot refrain from saying that our interest in our appearance is a sickness common to all humans created in God's image because we, deprived of the sense that justifies luxury, cannot conceal the fact that we too are stricken with this fever, which isn't even important, and which we must look at as being incurable. I will have to study in order to find a preventive to protect children deprived of sight who have not yet been conquered by vanity.

CHAPTER 10

Our Situation at the Table

Before undertaking a discussion of the Educational Plan that I promised to my young male and female comrades of misfortune, I must quickly speak to my readers about our situation at the table, which, I'll admit, is not the most satisfying thing for us. There are even days when the people with whom we eat invite their friends, then we voluntarily excuse ourselves from the meal because newcomers increase the pressure, and we must endure an intolerable discomfort.

Those deprived of sight who, like me, live surrounded by their families, eat with much more clumsiness than the blind raised at the Royal Institution [for Blind Youth], and here is the reason: I am convinced that people will find it both natural and specious. Those who are surrounded by relatives or by those who love them are very spoiled. People indulge them with an infinite number of small services, including cutting their bread, meat; one teaches them a terrifying idea of knives by forbidding their use; one is happy to be useful and agreeable [to the blind], and therefore they do not know, or at least rarely, how not to rely on the help of others at the table. Here is the origin of their difficulty in eating. One always notices an excessive embarrassment in them, as well as a clumsy air that adds further to the attention people pay to them. They know full well that it is to their mouth that they must bring what is served to them, but it is only painfully that they stick their fork, which they grip badly; when they attain a piece of food, they let it immediately fall onto their plate or even sometimes onto their clothing because their hand is always trembling. They eat soup, vegetables, eggs, milk products with even less ease. When they leave the table, they have as much food splattered on the outside of their bellies as other people have put into theirs.

But the dear creatures placed at the Royal Institution since birth are better taught than us, which protects them from our embarrassing conduct. They are watched with interest when they are in the dining hall. The touching looks of those who examine them are fixed on them and they hear their admirable intelligence praised, because luckier than we, thanks to their male and female teachers, they have learned to use forks, knives, and spoons with skill. I would like to copy them, but I am not sufficiently selfish to envy their lot; I urge them to be convinced, I entreat them to thank God each day for the advantages that He has given them; these advantages are too numerous for these kind blind people to justify their complaints about their situation, which seems to me to be even more pleasant than mine, although I lack their same talents. Nor do I have teachers who are as sweet as those who really want to teach them, and I haven't the hope to be directed by their indulgent and respectable chaplain who consoles them and encourages them to be patient. Being unable to aspire to more, I content myself with the affection that the people who surround me are willing to provide. However, I would be quite happy if the men and women who run the Royal Institution would deign to honor with their esteem the one whose only goal is to prove to them that her entire life will be filled with a profound respect for them.

CHAPTER 11

First Article of an Educational Plan Suitable for People Blind from Birth or in the Cradle

I shall divide my Educational Plan into several articles. I will first say in what manner one should raise a blind child until the age of seven. People think they are providing a great service to a child deprived of sight by satisfying all his wishes and caving in to his tiniest whims. The authors of his days reason more or less like this: poor child, he has so much to complain about that I can't refuse anything that he wants! Unfortunate parents! You think you are contributing to the happiness of your son or daughter, but alas! What is your mistake? Ultimately, you will not live forever, and this little being that you make into something unreal and haughty will one day be looked after by strangers. If you haven't taught him how to practice the humble submission that is extremely necessary for his status, he will be unable to stand the dependence he will be subjected to, and then he will curse your weakness as the cause of so many innumerable troubles that will burden him. Ah! he'll say, if only my father and mother had tamed the violence of my prideful character, I sense that my existence would be infinitely sweeter. You, who have given life to these noteworthy beings, be sure that they will not be unhappy, if you make them adopt sweetness and patience, qualities without which there is no happiness for them in this world or the next. Virtue will come easily to them, provided that they become familiar with it at a young age. Thus, put all your efforts into making them pious and resigned; I insist on this last advantage, which is necessary above all that they possess. Without resignation, there is no calm, without calm, no satisfaction, no bliss. Children deprived of sight must also be armed against all childish or even real fears. Their parents or their teachers would also do well not to blow the inconveniences of their situation out of proportion. On the contrary, they should attempt to show them that they are not unhappy. Nothing could be more useful than to inspire cheerfulness and pleasantness, which are absolutely necessary. For if they are lighthearted, they will certainly attract positive interest; if they are sullen, they won't be able to count on anything apart from a few signs of cold pity. If they are cheerful, people ask them questions, considering them as friends and with pleasure. If they are sad, people think they are doing them a favor by addressing a few insignificant words to them now and then. They are pitied, but are easily avoided. It is never without great difficulty that one takes care of these somber beings who can only give off feelings of being bored or even suffering from melancholy. But those who are blessed with a sweet vivaciousness, where their face lights up as soon as they hear a kind expression [and] who only reply to questions they are asked with a smile, patiently enduring their fate, and not complaining. I say these ones merit the interest that people are willing to show in them. Their company is pleasing, their conversation is charming, their quick wits are amusing, and their personality creates a tender feeling in all sensitive hearts touched by their situation. But their active friendship knows how to soothe their situation. Here then is my opinion on little blind beings. If their parents believe me, they will direct their [children's] hearts toward virtue, their souls toward reason, their feelings toward a resigned and agreeable philosophy, their judgment toward what is beautiful, good, and sublime, their minds toward the solid rather than the brilliant, by raising them without weakness and without too much strictness, in making them always hear the persuasive language of gentleness. Those to whom [blind children] owe their existence pave the way for joys as pure as they are unfailing. I wish them these joys in the name of the sincere affection that they inspire in me.

CHAPTER 12

Second Article of My Educational Plan

Here is the second article of my Educational Plan. I believe that it suits children entering adolescence, that is to say from seven to at most twelve years of age. As soon as a blind person becomes able to express himself, he must be taught to pray to God, his only hope and most reliable protector. It is necessary to refrain from teaching him anything else before he knows his prayers perfectly in Latin and French; since they should be familiar to him at the age of seven, he must be taught his catechism as well as a bit of grammar; it would also be useful for him not to ignore the fables of Lafontaine; until after his First Communion it seems to me that this is more or less all the instruction that he can acquire.

As for needlework, this depends more or less on the good will on the part of those who guide. That which one looks upon as vanity among those who see should be encouraged as a noble form of self-esteem among the blind. They must be forced to dress and undress themselves on their own, something that for them at first might seem difficult, but later they will end up getting used to it while thanking the authors of their days for having gotten them into a habit that will greatly reduce their state of dependence. It is not without imperious motives that I urge the parents of people deprived of sight to let them acquire a bit of a taste for luxury, for this is how they will have much greater pleasure in making themselves presentable, they will take care of themselves with admirable skill, and will end up by being useful to others. They care about their finery, which for them becomes a delightful occupation.

Furthermore, because it is proven that they have fewer distractions than those who see, it would be barbaric to deprive them of a pleasure that makes them appealing and amuses them at least for a while. They must be allowed to enjoy themselves, but with moderation. In talking to them about no matter what object, one must depict them such as they are in order to give them the possibility of getting a correct and reasonable idea of these things. Blind children must be taught the different names when giving them the toys that are customarily given to children. For us religion is a safe refuge, but one must be careful not to inspire in them piousness that is extreme because when they have reached the age of fifteen or sixteen they could become too fanatical. The people who look after the blind must be especially cautious in their conduct, for blind children do react to everything they hear. This is why the most exacting decency must be observed in their presence. Their parents shouldn't speak of the misfortune linked to their situation either, for if they know that they are pitied, they will become demanding, convinced that no one will refuse them anything they ask for, [and] every moment they will have new whims that it would be difficult, even impossible to satisfy. Rather than caving in to them, one should punish them as frequently as they deserve. It isn't in worshiping a child that one assures his happiness, especially when he is deprived of sight. I can't repeat enough to the people who gave them life not to raise [children] for themselves but rather for society, where they can, if they have virtues, belong. If the voice of a blind person promises to be sweet and flexible, one must try to teach him only verses that are incapable of attacking good morals or a few pious canticles in honor of the Holy Virgin and the saints. For every blind being, praising God is probably a very sweet satisfaction. I am certain that after having prayed, their pleasures seem more vivid to them. When the heart is pure and the conscience has nothing to hide, one can abandon oneself without restraint to the natural joys of youth as well as to the delightful feelings that these joys bring.

CHAPTER 13

Third Article of an Educational Plan

Now is the time for me to speak directly to young blind people because the third article concerns the ages from twelve to eighteen. I'd like to convince myself that they will easily understand me, and will listen to what I have to say with interest.

Oh my young and good friends! You, for whom I wish to end or lessen your difficulties, be on your guard against your own hearts, for they are almost always too sensitive, and can sometimes cause you incalculable harm for which there would be no greater hope for a remedy than for your situation. The people who direct and instruct you must make you aware of all the dangers that can result from an excess of overexcited feelings, which always come from works that, in the name of your peace of mind and happiness, I beg you not to hear. J. J. [Rousseau], Voltaire, and even Pigault, who is far inferior to them, should never strike your ears. In inflaming your young imagination, their novels would give birth in your hearts to emotions that at first would appear delightful to you and then would make you feel guilty or would give rise to regrets that will make you truly unhappy. Alas! I know only too well how easily our overly gullible souls can be tricked. We believe ourselves to be loved as we ourselves love, but those who are dear to us quickly disabuse us of this. Not being able to read faces, we have a better excuse than those who see when we attach ourselves to beings who don't merit it, and it is held against us infinitely more when our affections are betrayed. But the treachery of those whom we consider our friends makes us feel very cruel sorrows that we can avoid by keeping on our guard. Being less outgoing, we will be happier. I'm not saying, however, that we should live in a perpetual state of mistrust, which would make us sad and bothersome; I'm only pointing out that we should be more careful and prudent in our choice of a friend. We must not believe the affectionate words that one addresses to us because we do not see if his expression belies his tone. The sex that is not our own also obliges us to take greater precautions. It would do no harm always to remain a bit reserved with the opposite sex. Let us try to protect ourselves from attacks, which the sound of his voice or his mind can bring to our hearts. Suspicion toward him is permitted; if he shows an interest and expresses it in a frank and natural manner, we can sometimes take him at his word, but beware when we find him likable, for we can't suppose that we are loved; if on the contrary he addresses us with sickly compliments, we should hurry away from him, for we must not doubt that his intentions are suspect. If women who see are often tricked by men, what do we have to fear by allowing ourselves to be charmed and subjugated[?] I hope that our piety will make up for a strong soul, with which we don't all have the good fortune to be blessed. Oh, you whom I love and whom I like to watch as if a part of my family, follow the advice dictated by a tender and selfless affection, detest dangerous readings, flee from the company of frivolous and superficial people, and seek out that of worthy people! Cherish and practice virtue, and do good works [*bonnes actions*] without vanity [and] with the sole goal of being agreeable to God. Works by Riconboni, Montolieu, Cotin, Genlis, Barthelemy, and Ladot are as pleasing as they are interesting and educational. I am most convinced that you will like them very much. When I urge you not to become familiar with the works of Voltaire, I must, however, make an exception for his *Henriade*, as well as for the greater part of his dramatic works. Jean Jacques [Rousseau], without being the censor of religion and without writing against morals, does so, though, with too much passion. In these works one finds an exquisite sensitivity, which in agitating your young heads can become extremely dire. Avoid needing the help of others, but if it is absolutely necessary, show your appreciation, and never take advantage of the interest that people show in you. Don't let your heart be easily discovered, for you could regret it. I'm aware that our afflictions are independent of our will, but it is necessary to keep them in check as much as possible, taking absolute control over them; this will be difficult for us, but we hope to succeed, aided by our efforts and by the protection of Him who rules over all things. What glory for us! If this great enterprise is crowned with some success, how sweet will be the satisfaction we shall feel! Oh my God! In according us this success, deign to believe us worthy and inspire in us the necessary resignation religiously to accomplish your holy will.

CHAPTER 14

Fourth and Final Chapter on My Educational Plan

I am going to end this Educational Plan by indicating to young people of eighteen years of age how they should conduct themselves in order to live their best years without trouble and interior strife. I begin by giving my advice to a blind man. He, who in his eighteenth or twentieth springtime, feels the delightful beating of his heart when a pleasant woman draws near to him would do well to draw her attention to a gentle, modest voice, by exhibiting an extremely even temper, and finally by showing the brightness of a good character and sound mind. If, however, he is fortunate enough to possess these advantages, even if his situation in reality offers only a small number of inconveniences, but which more than one young woman would find intolerable, if those who love a man deprived of sight and are loved by him agree to unite their destiny with his, the latter must be grateful for this heroic sign of attachment, which those who see even call a sacrifice. May this word "sacrifice" not shock the people I am addressing, for I am far from using it with the intention of hurting them; I only want to show him that he should consecrate his life to embellishing that of this sensitive and dear woman who gives herself voluntarily to him. If, as I am sure, the conduct of the woman is decent, that of the husband absolutely must conform to that of his comrade, for whom he could do no better than to repay her kindness and care than with a boundless tenderness and an unconditional trust. May he beware of showing the slightest dissatisfaction or displeasure, even if certain actions of his wife should warrant it. May he always be even-tempered, his behavior delicate; may he not deprive the one with whom he is united of the pleasures conferred by her age and sex. May he never find a purer pleasure than in being pleasing to her, may he only apply himself to making her happy, may his conversation be educational and amusing; finally, if he has the good fortune of being a father, may he teach his children more through his example than through his ethics to cherish and to practice virtue. If these principles agree with his taste, and he follows them, so that after having led a gentle, happy, and calm life in this world, he will obtain eternal compensation in the next. It is of utmost necessity that a blind man take a female companion, because since he can't get around on his own, she becomes his guide, his protector, his guardian angel.

But we women, whose gender makes us naturally sweet and compassionate, being deprived of sight we can, even must, not associate our lot with that of men, for what pleasure could marriage possibly offer us? If we were to marry a blind man, then our situation would truly become sad because our husband's ideas would be as limited as our own. One of us could not offer great help to the other, and if Heaven were to send us children, we would be obliged to entrust them to strangers. And surely paid care does not equal that lavished by good parents; we could not enjoy their first smiles nor their touching looks, when they would be capable of using them to express themselves, and as a result if they were to make mistakes it would be difficult, if not impossible, for us to punish them. If we give them orders, only rarely would they obey, knowing full well, even being very young, that our position would seem to keep us from being very severe. We are thus obliged to rely on servants to dress, feed, and teach the people we have brought into the world how to live, and for their education we must rely on teachers whose affection is proportional to the pay they receive. Dear God! What care! What education! Poor children! Wouldn't you sometimes curse the people to whom you owe your existence?

If this portrait is horrifying, that of a young unmarried blind woman marrying a sighted man is even worse, for if she has any money, she shouldn't deny the fact that this would be his only motive for seeking marriage. In this first case, if she is weak or silly enough to accept proposals made to her, she must expect to be the most unhappy person in the world, for immediately after her union, the delicate attention, the careful consideration of the lover disappears, gradually, and is replaced by cold and disdainful indifference. The husband, who found admirable qualities of surprising intelligence while courting his companion, is now surprised to have been able to see her this way. The charm is dissipated, and he can't even see the reality. He doesn't see his spouse for who she is, he considers her a worthless and insignificant being, with a bitter irony he makes her feel her state of dependence, he only concerns himself with promptly spending the dowry of his young victim, whose golden years are consumed with tears and useless regrets; I admit this picture is quite bleak, but alas! It is but unfortunately too true. I beseech women deprived of sight but with some money to live and die keeping hold of their precious freedom, and to make worthy use of their possessions. They need not doubt that God will bless and protect them if they never stray from the path of honor and virtue.

CHAPTER 15

Continued from the Above

I stopped myself for a few moments, persuaded that I should divide this article of my Educational Plan into two chapters. I'm afraid that the last sentences of the preceding chapter have altered the pleasant and gentle serenity of women deprived of sight; I ask them to believe that it wasn't my intention to frighten them, but rather to make the case that they should profit from their independence, that they would be wrong to lose it even to the most handsome and kindest man in the world, for it is quite possible that he might not be the best. I believe I can not repeat enough to a young blind girl without fortune that she should not marry; I am sure that she would not succumb to this madness, unless she was totally lacking in common sense, for in marrying a blind man she would thus have nothing but her husband, no other resource but that of going to beg for her bread. As for a sighted man, he would never unite his fate with that of a woman deprived of sight if she didn't have a considerable dowry to offer him. But in the case where a man possessing eyes became the husband of a poor woman without them, he could only be a bad person or someone entirely stripped of resources who would soon oblige his companion to regret having loved him, and to curse their union. Horrifying prospect! May it never be that of young blind people; however, they could also be very unhappy if they submit themselves to the yoke of marriage. How many women who enjoy the light of day do not regret their happy youth? There are even those who wish to see the chain broken that attaches them to a man without principles, libertine, gambler, despot, and strange fellow; at least by remaining single we are certain not to run the risk of facing a comparable danger. We don't give birth to beings whose actions could sometimes make us blush. Nor do we see the intrigues and vileness of which our husbands or some people in our families could be guilty.

How many unfortunate mothers are pressured into seeing a despicable son, a young man with an empty head filled with hideous crimes, a being that they have carried at their breast, nourished with their milk, deposited on the scaffold! Now wouldn't this grief-stricken mother at the depths of despair envy our situation? Oh, my God! says this woman, why aren't my eyes closed to light, they haven't spared me from reliving this horrible spectacle again and again, the memory of which will drive me to my grave. Oh, my son! Why didn't Heaven deprive you of sight at birth? You see, my young and dear friends, if our position can't be considered a happy one, it nevertheless spares us the sad destiny of this sensitive mother of whom I have just spoken, as well as that of her son. A young girl blessed with a pretty face sometimes only lives from her charms; without morals and without delicacy, this poor creature grows old dishonored by those who led her to vice; she becomes an object of scorn for these unfortunates. A scourge of degraded humanity in her own eyes, abandoned and abhorred by her family, not having a true friend to dry the tears that regret and misery have drawn from her, this unfortunate girl looks in vain even for a rock on which to rest her head. We must be convinced that if she, a victim of debauchery, were to see a blind woman, she would say to her, "How fortunate you are! Your lot is quite preferable to mine! Ah! If, like you, I had lost my sight in childhood, I would not have fallen from the height of pleasure into the heart of what is most abject." Never, no never, I am content to say to all blind women, we will not be reduced to this degree of degradation. We will cherish and will always seek to practice you, oh noble and precious virtue that is constantly painted on the exterior as pleasing as well as seductive!

To return to the pleasures of our situation, I will give another striking example of the hardships that distress women who see. Parents who are rich marry an only and cherished daughter according to their hearts; these respectable authors of the days of this young woman give her free rein over their possessions; they live at home, at first the husband showers them with attention, consideration, and delicate gestures, but once he sees that he possesses their fortune, his conduct completely changes; the frenetic passion for gambling takes over in him, and he has no scruples about satisfying [his urge]. He spends days and nights away from home, he spurns the tender affections of his troubled companion and her parents. He becomes filled with despair, he ruins those who have so many rights to his affection, and then to add further to their troubles, he commits suicide. Then what future offers itself to the eyes of the spouse of such a monster? She sees her father and mother expire from pain and want, their death ordinarily precedes her own by a short period of time. If a blind woman were to approach her at her last moments lying on her scanty bed of straw knowing her situation of want, the dying woman would gather her strength to tell her, you must not complain of your lot; may these misfortunes that plague me teach you to enjoy life for, if like you, my eyes had been closed to light, I would not have been subjugated by the husband who now brings me death after having deprived me of my esteemed parents; all three of us would still live quietly and happily, using our riches to contribute to the happiness of others. Nothing is more true, we can sweeten, even embellish, our existence. Let us not forget this.

CHAPTER 16

Ways to Console All Blind Women

And so my good friends, haven't the portraits that I have just offered your imagination saddened and consoled you at the same time? I am sure that your sensitive hearts are made more tender by the fate of the victim of maternal tenderness, her guilty son has also stirred your compassion, you have consecrated a few tears for she who presents a horrible example of the consequences of libertinage. The unfortunate wife of the gambler must have also given rise to a painful feeling in you, but you must have said to yourself, never will the destiny of any of these criminal or suffering beings be ours. Indeed not, my young friends, for you have the right to hope for a calmer life, because free from reprimands and by doing as many good deeds as are in your power, your days will unfold in the midst of pure pleasures and endless true joys. Troubles, restrictions, boredom will not dare come near you; you will not become wives, but you will have female friends, because your sweetness, united with your solid virtues, as well as the pleasing qualities that will accompany a correct and ornate mind, will allow you to win sincere friends, who will have no greater pleasure than to demonstrate their attachment by providing you with innumerable distractions. They will always find you likable, because you will provide them with a goal, you will become confident that they are not guided by the same sordid interest that would motivate a husband, if, however, you have the misfortune of losing your title of "Miss." If you keep your title your whole life, as I'm convinced you will, you will not become a mother, but might not the child of a sister, [or] of a dear friend be able to win your heart? How rewarding for you to lavish tender caresses and to receive those of the child! How many charms you'll find in making him repeat your name, and to have him fall asleep in your arms, or placing him in the arms of a mother who is capable of taking care of all his needs, and to prove to him your gratitude in overwhelming him with care and signs of friendship! Growing older, the child who is not your own loves you, his parents teach him to listen to you with fear and respect. Since nature does not prejudice you in his favor, you correct his mistakes and do not spoil him. Punished and rewarded by you each time that he deserves it, this child who obeys your every command lets you win him over in a way that sometimes even his parents cannot. You will see to his education, you can make of him a likable and respected being who, reaching the age of reason, frankly confesses that you are responsible for the good qualities that he possesses. But if, as unfortunately too often happens, the object of your tender concern is vicious and heaps disgrace and dishonor upon his family, you will pity him, but his dishonor will not reflect badly on you; it doesn't force you to blush for having given him life; you are not continually the object of tyrannical persecutions from a cruel and unjust spouse; you delightfully enjoy the charms produced by an intimacy based on all social virtues. I would like to think that such touching considerations will greatly reduce the regrets of people deprived of sight. This idea electrifies me and makes my work easy.

It would be very satisfying for me to learn that I was fortunate enough to calm the sorrows of my dear female friends, from whom, in return for the feelings they inspire in me, I ask a benevolent indulgence of which I know I have the greatest need. Without pretensions and without vanity I will always use my glory to please them, as well as the persons who would do me the honor of reading what I have written. Our sensitivity makes any kind of attachment extremely necessary; this is why we hasten to form an attachment as soon as we are able to appreciate and to judge both the men and women who surround us. But our feelings must make us proud, [and] it is up to our conduct to make them noble; we should try, however, to rein in our affections and to keep a tight rein over them in a despotic manner. This expression may well seem a little violent, but I use it in order to keep my dear female friends from being ruled by their hearts, for this task must be exclusively entrusted to their reason, which I have no doubt will always guide them along the difficult paths of honor from which they will never stray because I am assured by their position and their rare merit. Consoling hope! No, I would not like to think that you are imaginary; I want to keep you because you are so dear to me. If I was so unlucky to lose you, I would vigorously ask of the Supreme Being to put an end to my days. Oh, my God! I would say to Him in a penetrating tone, if you change your mind regarding the hope of my being useful to my comrades of misfortune, there is no more happiness for me left on earth. Heaven, which, if we are worthy, should one day be open to us, is the brightest prospect that makes us feel an infinite charm in dreaming of the immortality of the soul. Our body, its crude envelope, will descend into the grave, but if it is pure, our soul will fly to the feet of the King of Kings to enjoy an ineffable happiness. What pleasure this idea gives us. Yes, Eternal Father, Divine Creator of the heavens and the earth, whose goodness is far superior to the beauty of Heaven and the brightness of the sun, we would like to convince ourselves again and again that all our thoughts come back to you, and being purified by you, will bring us the great recompense in the next world that we try to merit in this one.

CHAPTER 17

Author's Exhortation to Blind People

May people deprived of sight work to practice a solid, but not timid piety beginning with childhood. Exempt from fanaticism and ostentatiousness, may virtue always be dearer than life to them. Bring out the merits of others, even at the expense of your own; don't try to shine at the expense of those around you; flee from the company of slanderers and gossips, and be careful not to imitate them; don't lose control of your anger; avoid dangerous readings and frivolous conversations; associate yourself with decent people; follow exactly the advice that they deign to give you; make it your policy to be as useful to the less fortunate as you can; love and respect your parents and teachers; follow their smallest orders promptly; never mutter against them; don't give in to impatience; pray to God with fervor so that He accords you patience. Be gentle, enjoy contemplation and meditation; may your even temper always be evident. God will permit you to let an affectionate gaiety appear in you. May no jealousy or rivalry exist between blind people; may they find pleasure in praising each other; may they also not stray from the noble frankness that must form the basis of their character; may gratitude be their most lively sentiment. They should not abuse the goodness of those who are willing to instruct them. May the taste for finery not be taken to the point of excessive vanity; they are not forbidden from being inspired by a certain competitiveness that one calls self-esteem; but they must establish a worthy balance between this quality and the fault of which I have just spo-

62

ken; may they abhor pridefulness, may extravagance not
be a part of them, but nor should economizing to the
point of an odious parsimony; may the most scrupulous
decency animate their discussions as well as their conduct [*maintien*]. If boredom overtakes them, may they
make numerous efforts to overcome it, for I can't stress
enough that they not succumb to sloth, which is recognized as the mother of all vices. I also recommend that
they do not display too much sensuality, that is, they
should eat out of need rather than for pleasure. Oh, you,
for whom misfortune is a powerful lesson to every generous and sensitive being, you deserve the benevolent interest with which you are honored, but never take advantage
of it; may your reason always guide your spirit; never let
hotheadedness have the slightest power over your heart;
rein in your sensitivity; control it, but may it not be expelled by selfishness; fear your elation, for it must surely
give rise to a continuous distrust within you; don't seek
to avenge yourself, leave hate to the lower and vile souls;
try even to honor those who cause you pain in order to
conform to the maxims of the Gospel; may your faults
not make you an object of scandal; only put a small price
on riches and vain pleasures in this world. If someone allows you to go to the theater from time to time, ask to attend those [performances] based on pieces drawn from
holy writings. Spurn dangerous, insignificant, superficial, trivial stories [*bluettes*] that are not even worthy of
captivating your imagination; taking your inspiration
from history, dramas, melodramas, and tragedies will, I
am sure, distract and give you profound satisfaction. If
I can permit myself to be elevated to the level of a moral-
ist, I beg of you not to find me severe, [but] tender and

genuine friendship leads me to advise you to be pious. I am persuaded that only piety can sweeten your sorrows and enable you to live through them courageously. If I presently urge you to choose virtue over existence, it is because I have acquired the certainty that only virtue can lead you to happiness. Detest fanaticism and ostentatiousness, I say, for they can lead to despicable actions. If your devotion were to be too staunch, it would drive away your friends and those close to you; in knowing how to emphasize the merits of others you will win the high opinion of everyone; by avoiding slander and malicious gossip, you will be assured of not making any enemies. Finally, by maintaining a sweet disposition throughout your life, you will see it pass in a calm and agreeable manner, and you will await without fear the fortunate moment when your soul brimming with good qualities and other virtues will receive from the hands of the Almighty the immortal crown that you merit and which I wish you.

CHAPTER 18

Conclusion

At last I conclude this little brochure dedicated to a man of rare merits, whom I flatter myself into thinking will indulge me; less certain that my readers will indulge me, however, I permit myself to implore their understanding because of my situation and youth. My numerous efforts and the care I have taken and will always take in order to move and interest the public are motives that allow my request [for readers' indulgence] to be considered. If one finds my style to be incorrect, I wish to be pardoned, for, having taken up literature only recently, I am nothing but a most mediocre writer. If they please some of my critics, my works will become my only diversion [and] they will not experience the slightest interruption; if I am encouraged by a little success, I will try to merit one that is even more brilliant. I know that my work has numerous faults, but even so, I submit it to be published in the hopes that one will deign to give justice to my intentions, and will give me credit for completing a sustained and extremely difficult work. My aim was not stand out. I would be too happy just to obtain a few words of approval. If one wishes to show any sign of interest, one will make a few visits to my bookseller in order to obtain this brochure, which is a very weak piece of work, but whose subject can be of interest; may it bring a hefty reward to the publisher and be pleasing to those who will want to get to know it. I also wish for my male and female comrades some pleasure when this is read to them, that they will forgive me for mixing my life with theirs, and I even hope they like it. Surely to them I must seem a bit rash, but they will take into account the similarity of our situations. In taking my leave of them, as well as of my dear readers, I urge them to believe in the sincerity of my affection, and my strong desire to have been, and always be, agreeable to them. If they favorably receive my sketch about the blind I promise to thank them with future works: "Coliste, or The Heroine of Virtue," "Octavie and Angelina, or The Disastrous Effects of Clandestine Affairs," "Occupations of a Good Father, or A Collection of Educational and Amusing Stories," "Edmon and Malvina, or The Sojourn of a Young English Girl in France."

III.

Note on the Author's Youth

THÉRÈSE-ADÈLE FOUCAULT

Translated from the French by Lise-Hélène Trouilloud

It is not so much by imitation, but in the hopes of gaining my readers' indulgence that I decide to place this note as an introduction to my work.

Another motive, perhaps even more convincing, gave me the idea: my heart is in need of recognition, and it is to fulfill such a need that I will provide here some details on my youth. A few months after my birth, I was deprived of sight. I never had the joy of witnessing the kind smiles meant for me; all of nature's beauties are unknown to me. Up to the age of thirteen, however, I felt neither grief nor regret: my painful position invoked emotion everywhere. I was pitied; I was urged to be courageous and resigned. I was not touched, but surprised. I listened with distraction to the praises for my joy, responding to them with nonchalance.

Knowing nothing and desiring to know nothing, I lived in total ignorance, which should have alarmed my parents. But my family considered me an insignificant being whose needs had to be provided for. It was thought that, for me, the supreme good was to be dressed, fed, and at times flattered. This was true: I was satisfied, or at least I believed I was. But when alone, I would ask myself if my sisters, whose graces and vivacity were praised, should believe themselves to be happier than me.

Incapable of resolving such a question, and even less capable of pitying myself, I would answer in the negative. I would resent them, however, when they said to me, having enjoyed some pleasures in which I could not take part, *God! How brilliant that was! Ah! Dear, if you had seen!* I disliked such remarks as they would almost sadden me. I would be delighted when they were forced to renounce a pleasure to which they had been looking forward for a long time. I was not motivated by feelings of malice, but in hearing their disappointment, I would exclaim with joy, *At least tonight you won't say, Ah! If only you had seen!* My annoyance seemed so comical that it would promptly comfort them; they would laugh and accuse me of envy. Never would such sentiment take hold of my heart, but I feared feeling regrets.

In order to avoid them, I would attempt to embrace my own unhappiness, which I was starting to feel in spite of myself: my mood altered visibly; I renounced my gaiety and the pleasure that I found in others' company; I asked to be left alone. I would often be found in tears, taken by surprise. When asked for the cause of such tears, I would answer, passing my hand over my brow, *"I am bored!"* "Well, then! Why don't you amuse yourself? Come be with us." *"No, I would be bored!"*—even if you mean it, you are being impolite. "But perhaps, a walk . . ."

"*When I go on a walk, I am bored.*" Indeed, I was bored everywhere, and I admit that I must have wearied others.

However, people avidly indulged me, and I would hear repeated around me, *She is so unhappy!* These words distressed me, and my ear as well as my heart could not grow accustomed to them. It seemed unjust to me; when one referred to other young persons, I heard, *They are interesting.* I was in such a sad frame of mind when the ways of Providence allowed me to meet a person commendable as much by his birth as for his virtues, and who showed as much wit as good judgment. He had barely set eyes on me when he understood the source of my sorrow, and busied himself with finding the proper remedy to alleviate it. He would not speak to me in a tone of pity: the sound of his voice was so soft, so affectionate, and the consolations that he deigned to lavish upon me so touching that he filled my heart with attachment and gratitude. He did not pity me and would, on the contrary, point out the advantages of my situation: his solid piety would lead him to talk to me of a happier life, a life that I should desire. I would listen to him happily; my ideas seemed to become clearer, and my soul, which until then had been in a state of turmoil, was gradually elevated. I became aware of religion, felt the heavy price that one must pay, and learned at the same time that religion alone ought to be my guide and my comforter. The troubles that agitated me disappeared, and thanks to the kindness of my new protector, reason took a stronger hold of me. This generous mortal had already done a great deal in returning me to myself, but he helped still more by persuading my parents that it was absolutely necessary to think of my education.

He encountered resistance that he hadn't expected, but this failed to frighten him. According to my family, my state of blindness constituted an obstacle irreconcilable with my instruction. Such observations made my illustrious advocate smile. He spoke with admiration of blind youths educated in Paris, praised their talent, their intelligence, and pleaded my cause with such eloquence that he convinced them to place me in a religious institution. My parents kept their promise a few weeks later.

I found girlfriends and a family in the convent: everyone showed the most tender interest in me, which was prompted less by my condition than by how easily I learned and how well I behaved. How could I have not obeyed? I did not receive orders, but opinions.

When I was summoned to return to my paternal home, I felt a genuine sorrow from leaving such good sisters and kind boarders who had known how to succeed at making me forget that I was deprived of the joys of seeing them. Finding myself once again surrounded by my family, I sought only to show off the little knowledge that I had acquired. My fortunate memory provided me with rather pleasing words: I spoke of all with such fluidity that ordinary people thought me witty, while those who were truly witty laughed at my simplicity.

My sisters, who loved me tenderly, would, however, let me assume a certain superiority over them of which I was proud and which, at times, I abused. They liked praising me. It was maybe to such genuine affection that I owe the favor with which an illustrious family, who lived near our house, honored me. Madame la Marquise de *** deigned to invite me to visit her. I was received most graciously. As good-hearted as she was amiable and spiritual, she took it upon herself to explain all that was unknown to me. It was in her company that my judgment took shape and that I conceived the desire not to grow estranged from everything, [to no longer live] in an idleness that my condition could have excused, [a condition] I detested now that each day I was in a position to admire the charms of a brilliant and cultivated mind. I dared offer this lady a few poor rhymes; she pointed out their flaws to me with kindness, and told me how I needed to approach and work at such a difficult genre. Her daughter, who possessed her angelic virtues and admirable talents, undertook to give me piano lessons, which commitments linked to her status too often interrupted. Alas! I was not destined to enjoy such happiness and tranquillity for long. Monsieur le Marquis de *** was obliged to leave our town, and his entire family followed him. I cannot think of their departure without emotion. Oh dear God! If the prayer of an unfortunate touched your august goodness, dare I implore you on my knees to watch in all places over the noble protectors whom you granted me for too little time.

After their departure, it was again amongst the nobility that I found a benefactor. Monsieur le Vicomte de ***, who was then prefect of our department, welcomed me with the most touching kindness. I presented him with my latest work. He encouraged me, gave me the hope of someday performing in public, and intensified my desire to work. I was then twenty years old.

The following year, my parents having experienced considerable debts, I realized with sorrow that I was about to become a heavy burden on them, even though they did not make me feel it. I resolved to support myself by making a living. But what could I do? I was not enough of a musician; incapable of taking charge of manual work, I first experienced some anxieties about my own future, which soon dissolved. I conceived of the idea to launch myself into a literary career. I knew that I might fail. Lively, young, and endowed with a strong character, which I believe rare for my age, I was, however, not frightened by the obstacles. I declared that I wished to go to Paris. Such a project created as much surprise as terror in my family, who presented to me the many dangers to which I would be exposed. This time, I resisted the wise and many pieces of advice that I received. Putting all my faith in my resolve, I would not let anything change my mind. My parents gave me *two hundred francs* and saw me off with regrets. I pulled away from their embrace. If I committed an imprudence, as I now believe I did, I was cruelly punished for it. Arriving in the capital, I, who in the past had been so calm and whose life had been so uniform, nearly lost my mind in battling with sufferings of every kind. Isolated and misled in my interests, I soon became acquainted with the horrors of misery. Great God! You know that within my family I had never experienced imperious needs. Finally accepting the advice of some good and pious persons, I, however, did not let misfortune crush me completely. I worked courageously.

Already, I had a few works sold for next to nothing. In vain I would plead to the publishers who had acquired them to bring them into print; all would respond that it was too risky. Finally I started to work on *The Converted Jewess*. The publisher that took charge of it promised me it would be in print by the following winter. I pray that one forgives my unjust defiance, but I feared that he would not keep his promise—so many others had been made to me that I was perhaps allowed to have my doubts. During this time, I met a young blind man who lived off his own talents. Without being put off by my bleak situation, he generously offered to share his limited resources with me. Again, I lacked prudence since I put him in danger, he who desired to improve my lot by uniting himself with me. I did not hesitate, however, and our marriage took place immediately, to the astonishment of those who took an interest in me.

My novel, *The Converted Jewess*, was published—my name appearing alone on top as I was not married when I sold the manuscript.

I put an end here to these fastidious details, which I gave only to answer different questions that I have been asked by illustrious persons. The benevolence with which the nobility welcomed my work while letting me rely on their indulgence allows me to offer the respectful expression of my gratitude. It was their touching kindness that inspired the layout of this story. This production, object of all my care, is also that of all my hopes. As in my first work, one will likely notice a fair number of imperfections. Although I tried to apply the sage advice that I received, I admit that my position might have induced me to include some implausible details. But I beg my readers to forgive me and to pity me, and to continue their affectionate encouragement. Honored by such kindness, I will stop at nothing to try to become worthy of it. And the most pleasant reward for my numerous efforts will be the approbation of a class to whom I owe my education, the development of my weak talents, and most of all, my first successes.

IV.

REFLECTIONS ON A MANUSCRIPT, A LIFE, AND A WORLD

ZINA WEYGAND AND CATHERINE J. KUDLICK

What are we to make of such a woman, who at once thwarted and embodied the prevailing social values of her day? Drawing on archival sources as well as secondary scholarship in history and literature, the remainder of this book offers a context for gaining a deeper understanding of Thérèse-Adèle Husson's life and work.[1] Not only do we hope to fill in some of the details of her mysterious and perplexing life, but we also want to raise larger questions about how she might fit into discussions about the role of women, religion, disability, and notions of the self in the early nineteenth century.

One of the first questions that comes to mind, especially after reading the "Reflections," is to what extent Thérèse-Adèle Husson's observations and ideas were original. To be sure, the manuscript housed at the Parisian hospital of the Quinze-Vingts is the first text written by a blind woman about blind people and blindness in daily life, at least as far as we know. Prior to Husson's time, most works about blindness had been written by sighted people, particularly with the growing interest in the senses expressed by the Enlightenment *philosophes*. In 1749, for example, Diderot published his *Letter on the Blind for the Benefit of Those Who See*, a philosophical exploration of blindness largely based on his encounter with the Blind Man of Puiseaux, a reclusive, highly intelligent man who offered insights into perception.[2] Though Diderot's work generated much discussion and controversy while whetting the educated public's curiosity about blindness, it really wasn't about blind people as human beings; rather, it used the experiences of a blind man as a form of investigative data to launch a series of larger philosophical speculations about the role of touch and hearing in the accumulation of human knowledge.[3]

The nineteenth century brought changes in attitudes toward self-expression, writing, publishing, and reading that would help make it possible for someone like Thérèse-Adèle Husson even to conceive of writing her "Reflections." Together, the French Revolution, which highlighted the political rights of the people, and Romanticism, with its artistic celebrations of the simple life of the common person, opened up a new space in which writers from all walks of life could be heard. For example, the proliferation of workers' autobiographies in France and elsewhere during the early years of the new century demonstrated that people who had previously been ignored now aspired to tell their stories, and many even enjoyed modest successes with publishers.[4] In such a climate, and coming on the heels of the excitement generated by Diderot's writing, it's not surprising that a number of blind men—and eventually a blind woman outside mainstream Parisian culture—began to dream that a broader public might be interested in reading about blindness from the perspective of a blind person rather than a sighted one.

Accordingly, in 1828 Alexandre Rodenbach published the first French work to be written by a blind person about blindness, *Letter on the Blind Following That of Diderot.*[5] The title page mentioned his blindness to give his observations credibility because of his personal experience. Born in 1786 and raised in a family of Flemish notables, he attended a private school run by the great French educator of the blind, Valentin Haüy, in Paris. Two years after publishing his response to Diderot, Rodenbach ran for a seat in the newly formed Belgian legislature, where he would serve over the next several decades. Despite its author's more elevated class status, Rodenbach's work shared many features with Husson's "Reflections," including discussions of colors and the external environment, the education of the blind, and even thoughts about deaf people. Probably both Rodenbach and Husson had been influenced by many of the same forces, and had the young provincial woman been differently connected, perhaps the "Reflections," which she had written a few years before Rodenbach's *Letter*, might have appeared first. Published or not, Thérèse-Adèle Husson's manuscript differed from Rodenbach's by openly addressing questions related to womanhood.

Even as it broke new ground in providing a first-hand account from a blind woman's perspective for the benefit of other blind women, the "Reflections" followed certain literary conventions of the day. In particular, the manuscript drew upon a growing genre of books and pamphlets that outlined how girls should be educated. From someone such as Napoleon, who believed that "the weaker sex" must be schooled merely to raise sons worthy of the Empire, to Madame Campan and Madame de Rémusat, who argued that women should have knowledge in order to become better companions to men, discussion flourished regarding why and how girls of all social classes should be taught. Moreover, Husson wrote at a time when a growing turf war between convents and private secular boarding schools provoked numerous writers to explore the best ways that girls might receive a religious education in the decades before the state intervened. Coming in the aftermath of the Revolution, such discussions raised important issues with respect to religion and France's efforts to re-Christianize. They also forced men and women alike to think about what roles wives and mothers should play in creating a stable nation after some revolutionaries' aborted attempts to give women equal rights.[6] While Husson didn't overtly participate in these debates, the second half of her "Reflections" was probably inspired by the discussion; certainly her idealized, righteous blind girls helped maintain the status quo.

But how would Thérèse-Adèle Husson have gained access to such ideas? In the introduction we mentioned that the "Reflections," produced before the refinement and diffusion of Braille for tactile reading, had been written by scribes under the author's dictation. Several factors relating to both the form and content of the document suggest that the role of the individuals who helped

Husson was not simply limited to transcription. For one thing, the style often resembles spoken language, implying that it may have originated from numerous discussions. It's possible that even if these individuals didn't critique her work, they at least read it to her many times, and that this, along with other works they also read to her, may have influenced her thoughts. Most important, we imagine that these individuals engaged in a dialogue with her, and as a consequence, forced her to formulate responses to certain questions that otherwise might not have been posed. These conversations could have acted to replace what she herself lacked in experience, especially in the domain of education. We wonder, for example, who could have whispered in her ear the pompous title for her manuscript, whose references to a widely disseminated philanthropic literature addressing the underprivileged classes—the poor, workers, prostitutes, prisoners, deaf-mutes, blind people—are so familiar to anyone who studies French society in the first half of the nineteenth century.

In any case, outside her own experience of blindness, we must ask what inner or outer authority compelled and enabled Thérèse-Adèle Husson to offer her own learned counsel to young blind women and their families. Had someone read her a number of works addressing these questions, such as those concerned with girls' education, or did she rely on people in her circle for this information? Can we imagine that she had actually read the works she warned her young friends to avoid, or did she merely limit herself to parroting what the "good sisters" and the devout nobles who had taken care of her education had told her?

To take a specific example, it's highly likely that someone read to her or commented on the *Essay on the Instruction of the Blind* by Dr. Sébastien Guillié, director of the Royal Institution for Blind Youth in Paris from 1815 to 1821.[7] This work, which had three editions between 1817 and 1820, was actually sold in Thérèse-Adèle Husson's hometown of Nancy. It must have been known to those interested in her education and who provided her with ongoing support in her projects. Without a doubt, the words of her "Reflections" evoke the first part of Guillié's work, "General Considerations on the Mind and Character of the Blind."[8] And while the second part of Guillié's *Essay* addresses the "*instruction* of the blind" as it was carried out in the first Paris school, Husson makes her own proposal for an "*educational* plan" to young blind girls and their parents in the second part of her book. At the time, the terms *education* and *instruction* were not used interchangeably. "Instruction" encompassed a much larger intellectual scope that included knowledge of specific subjects such as history, geography, literature, philosophy, and the sciences. "Education," meanwhile, should also shape the mind but with the aim of improving morals through character building in order to prepare children for adulthood.[9] As a general rule, "education" mattered far more for girls than did "instruction." Since Thérèse-Adèle Husson was more interested in the fate of blind girls, it's not surprising that, unlike Dr. Guillié, she made a point of proposing an educational plan rather than a program for instruction. At the same time, however, she appeared to follow his blueprint for discussing these matters, a possible clue that she knew his work.

But even if the "Reflections" and some of Husson's subsequent observations seemed to conform to existing ideas in matters such as education, she definitely displayed a genuine streak of independence. That her own life contradicted much of what she wrote in her "Reflections," for example, gives cause for thought while suggesting that perhaps the young provincial was in fact quite savvy. Consider her advice to young blind girls never to marry. What should we make of her baldly stated views at a time when marriage was so important to a woman's identity that the "old maid" was considered "an anomaly; [. . .] a fallen existence: [. . .] a destiny without a goal"?[10] The average French girl began getting this message at an early age and from virtually every direction. Relatives, neighbors, local events such as dances or fairs, characters in children's stories, religious sermons, all reinforced the ideals of marriage and bearing children. In fact, many of the girls' schools set up in the early nineteenth century had this as their expressly stated goal. The message was so ubiquitous that it almost became second nature to equate womanhood itself with married life. Even though women authors writing on female education incited mothers to warn their young people against "the false freedoms of marriage," and even though they sometimes urged young women to marry only men whom they had "long examined and scrutinized from all possible angles with the calmness of reason," they still agreed in a general way that "solitude, which is not good for the man, would be lethal for the woman."[11]

A less prevalent but not insignificant narrative carried these ideas several steps further, ultimately celebrating the woman who either by religious avocation or some other moral reason chose not to cast her lot with a man. A certain Madame Mongellaz, whose work was published in 1828 and analyzed at length in a wide variety of newspapers, from the Catholic *La Quotidienne* to the women's paper the *Journal des Dames et des Modes,* defended the single woman in a manner not unlike the one chosen by Thérèse-Adèle Husson in her "Reflections."[12] "Let us believe that the woman who does not marry has more delicacy, more sensitivity perhaps, and more spiritual refinement than others," Mongellaz explained,

> not having found the man whose heart was made for hers, not having found principles solid enough to guarantee her happiness, she preferred isolation from a society not worthy of her. Or, faithful to the love that the bonds of marriage were to consecrate and whose ties death had broken, she had wanted neither love, nor marriage in her life any longer. Another, who was disgraced by nature and sought only for her fortune, had enough wisdom to evade Cupid's offers.[13]

Moreover, a Catholic country like France (particularly as it underwent a fervent religious revival with the restoration of the Bourbons to the throne) had long found places for single women in convents and religious orders. As nuns or lay sisters, they performed acceptable social roles outside the family, living a monastic ideal that celebrated virginity and the virtues of celibacy devoted to the service of others. Most likely Husson wrote her "Reflections" with such women in mind, not to mention with their aid and guidance. Per-

haps she had learned the value of being single from ob-
serving the nuns who had been so kind to her, and perhaps she hoped to impress them by showing how well
she had learned their lessons. Put bluntly, women devoted to the ideals of a single life made the "Reflections" possible both practically and intellectually.

But something deeper surely must have motivated
what was clearly the most passionate part of Husson's
manuscript: perhaps she had internalized a powerful
set of social taboos against disabled women creating
families of their own. Perhaps her own doubts and self-
hatred caused her to categorize herself among the un-
marriageable women whom Madame Mongellaz described as "those disgraced by nature." Even in the gen-
erations before Western science and medicine would
help legitimize eugenics as a form of purifying the
human race of imperfections, custom dictated that
women with disabilities should not marry. Not only
might such women seem unattractive or unappealing,
but, as prevailing views held, they ran the risk of being
unable to perform the basic tasks of wife and mother.
As the nineteenth century wore on, a lively discourse
among everyone from medical doctors to blind activists themselves corroborated these views, sometimes
embellishing them with seemingly legitimate "data."[14]
A blind couple posed an even greater danger, as noted
in the strict rules forbidding marriage among the blind
residents of the Quinze-Vingts enclave in Paris. The
regulations of the Royal Institution for Blind Youth
and Guillié's writings stressed the need for maintaining strict separation between the sexes to guarantee an
appropriate moral and disciplinary climate that some

believed had been challenged by revolutionary excesses. (His predecessor and founder of the Royal Institution, Valentin Haüy, had always encouraged marriage among blind people.) But like Husson, the administrators had little problem with a blind man who desired to take in a sighted woman as his protector or a blind woman who married a sighted man. Somehow, however, it seemed more likely that a blind man would have a sighted protector than a blind woman would, perhaps because priority was given to men who couldn't earn a living. Moreover, more places existed for blind men in the institution to begin with.

Despite such taboos, we know from both the preface to her *Story of a Pious Heiress* and from corroborating archival sources that Thérèse-Adèle married the generous blind musician Pierre-François-Victor Foucault in 1826. Why in the face of all these social pressures did she ultimately go against not only her own advice but also that of the influential pious people who protected her? Perhaps she had never allowed herself to dream of marriage as a young handicapped girl, and hence had written the "Reflections" in a fit of moral resignation. Perhaps she had intended to marry all along, and simply repeated what she thought people wanted to hear. Or perhaps the young provincial who had spoken from her heart out of religious conviction stunned even herself when she found her urban loneliness soothed by a man who welcomed her to share his small resources and life. As we shall see, her choice to marry would be viewed by many as a betrayal, and it would have serious consequences for her life.

·

A variety of sources in Nancy and Paris allowed us to piece together much of Thérèse-Adèle Husson's "true" story. To put it in context and perhaps even to find traces of her life that she chose not to discuss, we needed to understand something about the lives of other blind people living at the time. At first, this seemed an impossible task because, as with women, peasants, the poor, or anyone else with little power or influence, few blind people from any class left personal traces of their existence. Largely illiterate and overwhelmed by the demands of survival, those on the margins seldom enjoyed the luxury of recording their hopes and fears, joys or sorrows. Even among the better off, not everyone had the skills or the desire, let alone the means, to make their voices heard. Few, for example, could afford the services of a scribe or reader. Fortunately, many left indirect testimonials in the form of pleas for admission to an institution or by capturing the imagination of someone such as a priest, a benefactor from the nobility, or a city official who recorded their impressions.

Though Thérèse-Adèle Husson left an astonishing amount of information compared with other blind people living at the time, we had to be careful not to take everything at face value, just as we needed to cross-check certain assertions against other kinds of evidence. Besides the texts reprinted in this book, for example, we found information about her life in the forewords and dedications in three of her novels, all published by Belin–Le Prieur in Paris: *The Converted Jewess, or The Triumph of Christianity Followed by The Distinctive Orphan, or Piety, Suffering, and Courage* (1827), *The Book of Moral Amusements, or Virtue in Action* (1829), and *Story of a Charitable Sister*

(1830).[15] Dedicated respectively to a high dignitary of the Church, to the nobility, and to the Sisters of Saint Vincent de Paul, these texts provide intriguing details, but they belong more to the category of eulogy than to autobiography. As we'll see shortly, for example, it's possible that our author exaggerated certain aspects of her suffering upon her arrival in Paris to exalt the virtues of those who came to her rescue.

The content of Thérèse-Adèle Husson's novels themselves provides another revealing source of information, albeit one that must be handled with extreme care. Her writing touched on themes and plots characteristic of the Restoration period's most popular genres. As works of edifying juvenile fiction, her novels clearly intended to convey a message of piety and goodness to young readers. As a result, their moralizing messages touched on religion, sentimentality, education, and the virtuous return of the monarchy and nobility from exile after the French Revolution. Like the immensely popular fiction of authors such as Madame de Genlis, Madame Cottin, Pauline de Meulan (Madame Guizot), and other lesser-known writers who drew on some of these themes, Husson's books involved convoluted plots where after several untimely deaths and brushes with financial ruin, goodness triumphs over deception, the main evildoers are punished or converted, and a fragile young heroine either emerges victorious or dies nobly by teaching others valuable lessons in humility and fortitude. Such books were best-sellers in Restoration France, with Sophie Cottin's book *Claire d'Albe* outselling all others.[16] Thus, Thérèse-Adèle Husson's novels conformed to an established formula for literary success in the Restoration period, a fact that should make us cautious in attributing too much personal significance to how particular characters or plots unfolded.

Even so, certain moments in her novels might provide some insight into how Husson approached her world. Consider, for example, how she depicts blind people. Interestingly, very few blind characters appear in her fiction. But two works stand out: *The Three Sisters, or The Effects of Blind Motherhood* (1833) and the novella *The Young Blind Boys* (1838).[17] In *The Three Sisters* Laure, a young girl from a well-off family, is temporarily blinded but permanently scarred both physically and emotionally by smallpox. After her loving mother's premature death, her father remarries a woman obsessed with money and appearances. Upon helping Laure find a doctor to cure her blindness, the stepmother spurns her in part out of selfishness and disgust with her new daughter's hideously scarred face, but also because, truth be told, Laure is not a very pleasant little girl. Eaten alive with jealousy toward her beautiful sisters and their successes with male suitors, she complains bitterly that she is not attractive enough to marry, and sets out to create various intrigues to pit her sister against her half-sister, sometimes ruining a promising courtship or threatening a marriage once it's under way. Laure becomes an appealing person only by the end of the lengthy novel, after she has been forced to live a life of poverty sleeping on beds of straw in the garrets of Paris. One can't help but wonder if Thérèse-Adèle hasn't in fact created her own evil alterego in the ugly, difficult, demanding, manipulative, but ultimately redeemed Laure. While this fictional character doesn't provide much information about blindness, we can feel the anger that surely must have consumed her because of smallpox. Like her antiheroine, Thérèse-Adèle had herself gone blind because of this common disease (though she didn't recover her sight), and most likely she suffered much because of the serious scars it left behind.

The only other blind characters appeared in a later novella, *The Young Blind Boys*, a work published after her death. Blindness serves as a plot device to show how goodness is usually bestowed by pious people who have internalized the upstanding values of Catholicism. The story opens with a group of depressed noblewomen living in exile just across the French border in Koblenz. They are cheered by the sweet sounds from a blind man's violin playing, which prompts one woman to embark on a long and convoluted story of two likable blind teenage boys who had received help from her now deceased husband as they wandered through France during the turbulent revolutionary decades. They have been set loose by an evil stepmother who doesn't wish to care for them. With no skills and little money, they roam the countryside, where they are alternately duped by unscrupulous innkeepers and saved by the religiously inclined. Eventually a fleeing convict, a good fellow, befriends them, urging the lads to allow his son to serve as their sighted guide in order to give him a real purpose in life. Together the three travel the countryside, finding various good souls who invariably rescue them from misadventures with evil people by offering them lodging and menial jobs until either difficult financial circumstances or an untimely death (usually from a protracted ailment) forces the lads to move on. Eventually, they end up at the home of the émigré narrator and her husband, where the three impress their hosts with their piousness and sincerity as well as their strong desire not to become a burden.

While the blind characters served as the center and pretext of her stories, Husson had a complex relationship to them. On one level, her heart didn't seem to be in describing blind people or blindness. Her depictions in *The Young Blind Boys* gave little indication that the blind characters had been created by someone with any personal connection to it; if anything, they conformed tenaciously to stereotypical descriptions of the blind in literature, with blindness serving as a stock plot device to highlight the pure good or pure evil of various characters they encountered. Perhaps she chose to provide descriptions that people expected to read in order to reach a wide popular audience. Or maybe she wanted to distance herself from these characters in some way, protecting herself from sadness and anger but also allowing herself to dream a little. To be sure, as boys and as a twosome (and eventually a threesome) they enjoyed the freedom to travel through the French countryside usually denied to sighted women, let alone blind ones.

But on another level, perhaps Husson peppered her stories with a few precious details from her own life. We can appreciate this more fully when examining moments in her novels that stand out for their passion and raw emotions, writing that seems uncharacteristic of her mostly distant and almost formulaic style. Such passages cry out to the reader in a way that gives us pause to wonder if for a brief time—and even unknowingly—our author had tapped into a deep inner reservoir of past feelings. Her *Story of a Charitable Sister*, for example, contains a heart-wrenching scene in which the young heroine (named Adèlaïde) learns of the death of her protector, the Baroness de Gerville. With Adèlaïde we overhear the baroness as she calls for a notary and a priest. When the poor girl can stand it no more, she forces herself into the room where her protector lies dying. Overwhelmed with emotions, and heartbroken at hearing her young charge's sobbing, the older woman has her removed from the room a second time. But again Adèlaïde can't stay away.[18] It's easy to imagine a young Thérèse-Adèle going through a similar scene with one of her own noble protectors, thereby giving a sense of how deeply she felt about the interest they had taken in her. Again, we must be careful not to read too much into these scenes, since they were produced for a literary market adhering to definite rules to guarantee success. But taken together with other sources, they can offer important insights into how the young girl must have felt.

To fill out Thérèse-Adèle Husson's own narratives, we turned to less lyrical but more specific administrative documents such as birth and baptism records, marriage licenses, pleas for financial assistance, judicial files, police reports, hospital and hospice records (particularly files documenting admission requests, letters of support for admission, medical certificates, and legal papers), charity rosters, publishers' ledgers, and requests for publication rights.[19] Some traces seemed hopeful but went nowhere, while others yielded intriguing surprises or provided new clues to follow up that led to still other discoveries. For example, something seemingly innocuous like a marriage certificate provided not only the names of the newlyweds but also those of witnesses and an indication of how literate a person may have been based on the quality of handwriting used in the signature. Read against records that listed the address of the signer, such details led to revelations about the extent to which the Husson family was connected to the local community and to which social class they belonged. But even with such detective ingenuity, our narrative remains speculative because certain details will forever remain obscure.

Born in Nancy on the 14 pluviôse, year XI (February 4, 1803), Thérèse-Adèle Husson grew up in an environment that had changed little since the events of the 1789 Revolution and the rule of Napoleon, a world that struggled to reconcile past and present by turning back the clock. The city had long been an important administrative and commercial center in eastern France, housing a bustling population of approximately 30,000 people, 10 to 15 percent of them artisans and shopkeepers. Emerging after 1814 from the turbulent years of revolution and war virtually unaffected, Nancy continued its role as the garrison town it had played during the Old Regime, the place Stendhal described in the first part of his unfinished novel, *Lucien Leuwen*.[20] In fact, the restoration of the Bourbons to the throne in 1814 had helped return France to a time when the Catholic Church again reigned supreme. Secure in their convictions that once again their country belonged to the pious and the wealthy, members of the nobility who hadn't been executed or bankrupted during the revolutionary Terror could return from their exile abroad.[21] Shaken but not dramatically affected, the nobility of Nancy continued their lives reassured that once again they were in tune with the nation.

But even as residents of Nancy returned to the calm of the Old Regime, important changes in the religious climate would influence Thérèse-Adèle Husson's life and writing. The year she was born, the local administrative prefect, M. Marquis, and the bishop, Monseigneur d'Osmond, agreed to reconstitute a number of congregations that had been dispersed by the Revolution, including female religious orders with a teaching vocation. Such women would be instrumental in Thérèse-Adèle's instruction. Among them were the Sisters of Saint Charles, founded in Nancy during the seventeenth century, and the Sisters of Christian Doctrine, an order founded in Lorraine during the following century.[22] The bishop and the prefect also agreed to practice political tolerance toward non-Catholics.[23] Here it's useful to note that as early as 1788, Jews had obtained permission to open a synagogue on the rue de l'Equitation (the street where the Husson family lived), but only in the middle of a courtyard separated from the street by a tall structure so that their ceremonies would not be seen or heard by passersby.[24] In this same neighborhood an old church, l'Eglise des Prémontrés, became Protestant with Monseigneur d'Osmond's permission in 1806.[25] One wonders how the proximity of these religious sites was viewed by the Catholic population of this neighborhood of artisans and storekeepers where many Jews had lived since the eighteenth century. We also wonder how the "good sisters" who raised Thérèse-Adèle Husson and the devout members of the nobility who enlightened her with their advice felt about Monseigneur d'Osmond's tolerance toward non-Catholics. In any case, the presence of a synagogue and a Protestant church in the neighborhood of her childhood perhaps influenced the themes that she chose to treat in her first novels: the conversion of a young Jewish woman taken in by a noble family during the era of Louis XV (*The Converted Jewess, or The Triumph of Christianity*), and of a noble Protestant during the era of Louis XIII (*Story of a Pious Heiress, or The Happy Result of Confidence in God*).

Both of these novels were inspired by the Catholic zeal to reclaim France for both church and monarchy after nearly a quarter century of revolution. The events and spirit that accompanied this re-Christianization effort had an impact on every French person living at the time, drawing them into unforgettable public displays of religious fervor. In its most dramatic incarnation, the revival consisted of huge public prayer meetings known as "Missions to the Interior," which reached a climax in the years Thérèse-Adèle Husson passed through puberty and into adulthood. Thousands of these occurred in France between 1815 and 1830, many of them drawing several thousand people to public places, where they would erect crosses the size of buildings and distribute religious literature.[26] Monseigneur de Forbin-Janson, the cofounder of the Society of French Missions between 1814 and 1816 who succeeded Monseigneur d'Osmond after his death in 1823, was one of its most ardent zealots and someone who would play a future role in Husson's life.

Thérèse-Adèle Husson came from a family of the lower-middle classes. At the time of her birth, her forty-nine-year-old father, Marc Husson, was a carpenter; he died five years later. A directory of Nancy's population for 1807 indicates that Marc Husson, a native of the city, lived with his family in the house he owned in the neighborhood of Ville-Neuve on 331 bis rue de l'Equi-tation. At this time his family consisted of his wife, Anne Millot (also born in Nancy), their eight children (the youngest being seven days old), and a servant, Anne Catherine Lallemand.[27] Thérèse-Adèle's father had a brother, Pierre, who also worked as a carpenter and who lived on the impasse des Artisans, not far from the Hus-son family's street.[28] Possibly the two brothers worked together in a family workshop passed on to them by their father, the late Sigisbert Husson, a master carpen-ter. Anne Millot, Thérèse-Adèle's mother, was both the daughter and the sister of merchants. On Anne and Marc Husson's marriage certificate of April 24, 1787, there also appears a certain "Pierre Barbier, printer and bookseller, maternal uncle of the groom."[29] Several decades later an individual named Barbier can be found in the printing business living at 13 rue Saint-Jean, a street perpendicu-lar to rue de l'Equitation. Such a family affiliation with printers might have played a role in Thérèse-Adèle's vo-cation as writer, even though we have no way of confirm-ing this. In any case, she belonged to a lower-bourgeois family of artisans and shopkeepers, circumstances in which she admitted that she had never suffered from want. Ten months after the death of her husband, which occurred on October 2, 1808, Thérèse-Adèle's mother married a widower, Joseph Martin, a policeman who lived on the rue de la Révolution, a few hundred yards from the rue de l'Equitation.[30] In 1820, we find that Joseph Martin, Anne Millot, and their respective children had moved to the rue du Pont Mouja, still in Ville-Neuve but this time in the neighborhood around the cathedral where Joseph Martin owned a house.[31] Thérèse-Adèle never alluded to her father's death nor to her mother's re-marriage in her autobiographical texts. However, several of her novels do describe similar situations that posed distressing problems for the children involved.[32]

According to her "Reflections," Thérèse-Adèle became blind at the age of nine months as the result of smallpox. At the beginning of the nineteenth century this fairly common disease represented one of the leading causes of infantile blindness despite public officials' efforts to encourage vaccinations.[33] From her own account, we learn that she didn't suffer much from the consequences of her disability until adolescence. She might have been neglected by her mother and stepfather, since she attributed the major crisis of depression she suffered during puberty to the fact that, knowing nothing about possibilities for educating blind people, her family allowed her to languish in a state of idleness. Whatever the cause, this crisis was to decide her future. During her depression the "illustrious figure" whom she mentioned in the "Note on the Author's Youth" took an interest in her case and convinced her parents to place her in a religious school where she would finally receive the instruction she had gone so long without. We know that in order to gain the family's acceptance, this enthusiastic man praised the talent and intelligence of the young blind people being educated in Paris. In her "Reflections," Thérèse-Adèle evokes the "dear creatures placed at the Royal Institution since birth," knowing of it only by hearsay. It's possible that her high opinion of these students would influence her feelings toward her future husband because he himself attended school there.

While Husson failed to provide details regarding the

religious house that educated her, we discovered a number of likely candidates. The Sisters of Saint Charles, who had returned to Nancy in 1803 after their banishment during the Revolution, ran a girls' school just a few blocks from her childhood home.[34] Slightly further away, the Sisters of Christian Doctrine returned the same year, reopening their school located in Ville-Neuve, which by 1808 had admitted 250 students.[35] However, both of these were day schools usually attended by poor girls. Not only did Thérèse-Adèle describe her family as being reasonably comfortable, but she also claimed that she lived at the school. Was she then put in the care of the Visitandines, who ran a boarding school in Nancy during the Napoleonic era and the Restoration before returning to a purely contemplative vocation?[36] Since the archives of these congregations from Nancy are unavailable, we'll never know. Nonetheless, it's worth pointing out that the Sisters of Saint Charles, who ran the school just a few blocks from the Husson family's home, would assist the Abbé Gridel, the founder of the Institution for the Blind Youth of Nancy in 1852.[37] Would these nuns, whose congregation was the region's major charitable association in the nineteenth century, already have shown sympathy toward blind people in the years 1815 to 1820 by accepting to be the "good and charitable mistresses" of Thérèse-Adèle and her friend Charlotte? If so, Husson would have been embellishing the truth by pretending to have been educated in a boarding school.

Judging from the testimonies of women writers of Husson's time, female education was generally of mediocre quality, regardless of the type of school. Even one of the most elite girls' schools of the day, the convent of

Sacre Coeur in Paris, didn't have the best results. One student, the noblewoman Marie de Flavigny, recalled how in one of her advanced classes only two out of five knew how to spell correctly.[38] Meanwhile at the convent of the Augustines Anglaises, George Sand would rate the quality of her studies as "more or less a zero."[39] Classes tended to be watered-down versions of male subjects intended to instill good religious values rather than actual knowledge. One school, for example, described the goals of its course "Philosophy for the Benefit of Young Girls," which involved "studying religion with justifications and precise responses to the most common objections" and remaining "on guard against the futilities of an existence without goals and the dangers of novels, performances, grooming [*la toilette*], and cackling in salons."[40] Such learning tended to require more memorization than understanding of the facts, since for the most part current educational theories—in convent schools as well as their secular counterparts—held that women should be educated in order to function well in polite society and to instill knowledge and good morals in their sons.

Though her "Educational Plan" didn't radically depart from many of these values, Thérèse-Adèle later expressed some frustration in her "Note on the Author's Youth." Here she decried her limited instruction and the need for her "fortunate memory," which later "provided her with rather pleasant ideas" to share in society. Thus, despite her gratitude toward the nuns who had known how to make her forget her blindness, Husson admitted that she only began to learn once she had left their care. She claimed that she formed her judgment in the company of someone she described as "la Marquise de ***" who had "deigned" to further her education when young Thérèse-Adèle returned home to live with her family. The same noblewoman had agreed to guide her first literary steps, after having introduced her to several new areas of knowledge. Thus, even though she came from a modest family background, Husson in effect received a private education much like that of many noblewomen. We wonder if such opportunities would have been available had she not been disabled, since the good marquise was engaging in a socially sanctioned act of giving charity to the poor and blind. At the same time, we can't deny that Thérèse-Adèle surely must have displayed enough intelligence and hunger for learning that an accomplished noblewoman would have been drawn by these qualities as well.

When, much to her despair, Thérèse-Adèle's protector left Nancy, she once again found a benefactor within the nobility in the person of "Monsieur le Vicomte de ***, who was then prefect of our department," to whom she presented her first work. Despite the mystery with which she surrounded the names of the noble figures who came to her rescue (not an uncommon practice at the time), we suspect that one was Vicomte Jean-Paul Alban de Villeneuve-Bargemont, prefect of the Meurthe department from May 21, 1820, to October 11, 1824. A fervent supporter of the religious revival and the Bourbons' return to the throne, he foreshadowed a more benevolent kind of social Catholicism that would take up the causes of poverty, working conditions, and disability in the coming decades. His work on political economy inspired by Christianity remains known to historians even today.[41]

According to the "Note on the Author's Youth," when Thérèse-Adèle turned twenty-one the Husson family found itself in financial straits. So as not to burden those around her with her "useless mouth," the young woman decided, as she put it in her own words, to "support herself." But she was not destined to follow the traditional paths trod by blind people before her. Believing herself incapable of manual work and finding herself not enough of a musician to earn a living, she resolved to live off her writing, as did several other lower-class women of her time who "launched themselves into literary careers by necessity."[42]

And like so many other aspiring provincials at the time of the Restoration, she headed for Paris. Whatever fascination the capital exercised on the provincial youth of the time, it was a rather surprising decision for a young woman, since only young men usually risked setting out for the great French metropolis. For the most part, women remained in the provinces, a place of "compressed fervor" where they found themselves buried alive by what writers of fact and fiction alike frequently described as a socially oppressive climate, a situation later conveyed so well by characters such as Flaubert's Madame Bovary. Meanwhile, Balzac's characters have taught us to appreciate that the capital's hold on provincial minds was a mixed blessing.[43] His novels such as *Old Goriot* and *Lost Illusions* depicted ambitious, scheming social climbers who forgot their provincial families as the glitter and power of Paris seduced them. And such dreams could lead to success just as easily as they could end in devastating failure. What a challenge for a young girl, especially as a blind person, to leave the comforts of home life in Nancy and take her chances in Paris! If, as she wrote, the members of her family did everything they could to hold her back, we can imagine that Thérèse-Adèle had to show strong resolve to convince them to allow her to set off on her journey.

Husson probably had to defend her decision with numerous arguments, among them, no doubt, the promise of one day obtaining a coveted pension from the Quinze-Vingts hospice, thanks to the recommendation of some noble protector. Regulations introduced on March 14, 1801, allowed for 420 blind people to receive support.[44] Those admitted fell into one of two categories: the first consisted of 300 men and women, age twenty-one and over, who could occupy individual dwellings that they shared, if applicable, with their spouse and children; the second consisted of 120 children, boys and girls from seven to sixteen years, who lived in a dormitory separated by sex, and, after 1815, housed elsewhere in the city. The adults, or "the blind of first class" who lived at the hospice, were called "internal members." They received clothing (which could be reissued every other year), a daily portion of bread and meat, firewood, and a stipend of thirty-three centimes a day, which altogether corresponded to a daily total of ninety centimes. In addition, the residents' sighted spouses and children would be supported, receiving a daily portion of bread along with other residents. If a blind person was admitted into the first class category, but preferred to live outside the enclave of the hospice, she could receive the thirty-three centimes a day but lost all other benefits relating to her admission. Those who chose this option were called "external members."

Blind People from the Quinze-Vingts Going for a Walk, lithograph by Jean-Henri Marlet, in Jean-Henri Marlet, *Tableaux de Paris* (1821–24).

Though living in the institution had the definite advantage of sparing the lucky pensioner many of the hardships of daily life in the capital, it's unclear if our ambitious young woman from the provinces would have been completely happy there. With the growing conservatism of the Church under the Restoration, the Catholic administrators of the Quinze-Vingts began imposing more strict regulations over their residents beginning in the early 1820s. First, the admission requirements to the hospice became more rigid than ever, especially regarding the requirement that residents demonstrate complete and incurable blindness. To this end, officials organized medical examinations to single out those who were not completely blind. This led to some of the residents being expelled, a rather arbitrary decision, given the absence of technical means to evaluate visual acuity and the field of vision at the time. In addition, the more conservative administration now required a certificate of Catholicism to ensure residents' piety. To complement this, officials subjected internal boarders to heightened surveillance to evaluate their moral and religious practices, at the same time that they called upon them to participate in public religious ceremonies. On December 1, 1823, for example, the Grand Chaplain announced that there would be a Mission to the Interior carried out during the following month for the blind of the hospital. Expecting "the most favorable results," the official judged it necessary, "given what religion has endured in recent times."[45] Moreover, in a confidential report to the Grand Chaplain on June 30, 1824, La Croix d'Azolette expressed horror at the presence of "two or three Protestant families in our holy asylum" and wished "to find a way to relocate those [Protestant] religionaries [whose] presence in our House is pernicious for this establishment."[46] Years later, a blind Protestant named Daniel Heilmann would attest that he had to leave the hospice "during the time of the Grand Chaplaincy [. . .] having [then] preferred sacrificing what was in his interest rather than submitting himself to recanting [his religion]."[47]

Finally, to crown its plans for controlling the residents, on January 10, 1825, the administration decided to require them to wear a uniform. Up until this time, interns had been provided every other year with the necessary fabric to have an outfit made of their own choosing. For men, the new uniform would consist of an outer coat, a jacket and pants in iron-grey colored cloth, with royal blue cuffs and collars, and copper buttons decorated with a fleur de lys (the symbol of the monarchy) and the numbers 15-20, for "Quinze-Vingts." Women were to wear a dress of printed linen and a blue belt decorated with a fleur de lys.[48] This reform, which would trigger much resistance, clearly fulfilled the objective of policing individuals in order "to easily supervise the blind of both sexes, in town as well as in the enclave."[49] The uniforms would also help the administration in its quest to prevent blind pensioners from "disgracing the royal asylum in which they lived" by begging in the streets or by practicing other illicit and degrading occupations such as "playing music at balls and in bars; singing or selling songs in the streets and in public squares; [. . .] telling fortunes, dealing cards, etc."[50] Interestingly, these uniforms harkened back to the institution's founding in the Middle Ages; in this earlier incarnation, however, the uniforms with the yellow fleur de lys were coveted because they gave their blind wearers the right, indeed the royal duty, to solicit alms for the blind community.[51]

The administration further sought to improve the public image of blind people by encouraging them to work in respectable jobs. To help pensioners who wished to supplement their modest stipends, in 1825 officials at the Quinze-Vingts drafted an "Inventory of the Various Arts and Occupations [Already] Exercised among the Residents" that would suggest more wholesome employment possibilities for blind people.[52] This study gives some idea of which professions French society viewed as compatible with blindness at the beginning of the nineteenth century, while suggesting which activities the administrators considered morally appropriate. The list recorded twelve wheel spinners (for tool sharpeners), one organ blower, one bell ringer, two water carriers, one lock picker, and one dispenser of holy water. Others required some skills, such as one master of grammar; one professor of mathematics (probably two former student-teachers of the Royal Institution for Blind Youth who had become members of the Quinze-Vingts and who had continued teaching outside the institution); one master of the English language (not a former student—a man who most likely exercised this profession before becoming blind); three clock makers; one toy maker; one sandpaper maker; one chair caner who made doormats; and one purse maker (most likely a former student of the Royal Institution for Blind Youth, where this profession was taught to girls). In addition, the inventory listed those who owned a store within the hospital grounds: two wine sellers, two tobacco and grocery sellers, one semolina and vermicelli seller. Finally, most of the working blind were musicians (twenty-three men and nine women), to which we must add two organists, who, for no apparent reason, occupied their own place on the register. The administration counted a total of 68 blind individuals "working or retailing" out of 225 members present at the hospice in February 1825, including 15 in the infirmary who were therefore unable to work. These listed occupations, some deemed "meager breadwinners," didn't allow someone to be self-sufficient financially, though they could certainly supplement the modest sums that the Quinze-Vingts provided for its blind charges. But without the institution's daily portion of bread and a small stipend they couldn't survive off these jobs. In light of all these possibilities, it's no wonder that Thérèse-Adèle fixed upon the Quinze-Vingts as her destination in Paris despite stricter regulations, and why she put so much effort into her "Reflections" to win over La Croix d'Azolette. It also helps explain why her parents would have been put more at ease by her departure.

We don't know if she traveled alone or if some kind soul agreed to accompany her through the rugged terrain that separated eastern France from the capital's waiting mysteries. If she traveled alone, she would have had to depend on someone to guide her, since the widespread use of white canes or dog guides for independent mobility was still more than a century away. The journey would have been a difficult one, taking several days in a series of rickety stagecoaches crammed full of passengers, many of them like Thérèse-Adèle carrying the sum total of their worldly possessions with them in awkwardly perched trunks. At night the coaches stopped at roadside inns, where a woman traveling alone would have seemed vulnerable or suspect, since such public spaces were increasingly becoming the domain of men. It's possible that our heroine suffered some ill-treatment at the hands of dishonest innkeepers, since her novels contain several descriptions of travelers being preyed upon. In what may be the most revealing, *The Young Blind Boys* offers a stirring account of the two travelers who are cheated out of the small amount of money they had been given upon leaving home. Naively, they pay an innkeeper for their first night's lodging, only to be told by his wife that they hadn't in fact paid. "You probably think that just because you're deprived of sight that you have to be fed and lodged for nothing," the woman snarls, and threatens to call the police when the fourteen-year-olds claim to have given over all their money, leaving them nothing with which to pay (p. 226). They, perhaps like young Thérèse-Adèle herself, were saved by a religious figure who happened to be passing through town and took a kind interest in them.

What must the young blind woman newly arrived in the crowded, smelly, noisy, jostling, dirty, narrow streets of Paris have thought? Husson embarked on her odyssey just at the time when writers, social commentators, physicians, and public health officials began to decry the capital's accelerating and seemingly inevitable decay. Piled high with both animal and vegetable refuse, the dusky streets were difficult to navigate for residents and the numerous horses that hauled heavy loads. With a sewer system still decades away, contemporaries described impoverished central districts where gutters ran with blood and debris from slaughterhouses, human waste, and mud, places that were dark even at noon on a summer day. Rotting food, urine, and horse droppings combined with burning coal and refuse to create a smell so foul that health officials dubbed these areas "homes of infection," which they believed caused periodic outbreaks of epidemics from dysentery to mysterious illnesses described only as "fevers."[53] To compound the crisis, in the 1820s the city was undergoing one of its most dramatic spurts in population growth, much of it due to arrivals from the provinces. Particularly in the working-class neighborhoods in the center of the capital, where young Husson would have arrived first, population density increased as the newcomers found themselves forced to stay within the city's ancient fortifications, where they would be more likely to find housing and jobs. And despite the population explosion, very few new buildings were being constructed to accommodate the new arrivals; according to a statistical survey published at the time, between 1817 and 1827 the city's population increased by 25 percent while the housing stock grew by only 10 percent.[54] Such conditions stood in sharp contrast with the wealthier neighborhoods to the west and in the outskirts, where Husson may have made an occasional visit, perhaps to one of her benefactors.

We can imagine that more than once our young traveler, faced with all this, must have had her doubts. Did she dream of jumping on the next carriage and heading home? Or did she really believe that once having left all she knew, there was no turning back? Did she stay in Paris simply because there was nothing left to lose, because she couldn't face the humiliation of giving up, or because she simply couldn't afford to pay for a return trip? Or did she believe deep in her heart that this is where she could realize her dreams?

We will never know the particulars of how young Thérèse-Adèle made her way from the stagecoach to what would be the first of many residences she would occupy in different Paris neighborhoods over the next several years. Records kept in the Quinze-Vingts' archives reveal that she was chosen to be an external pensioner there on December 1, 1825, retroactive to July 1.[55] In all likelihood, the "Reflections" she had dedicated to the Chevalier de La Croix d'Azolette, along with a letter requesting a pension and one or several supporting letters of recommendation, had done their job. However, since we could never find her actual petition and its supporting evidence, we don't know exactly what she wanted from the Quinze-Vingts.[56] Perhaps she initially requested an external pension because she hoped to live more freely outside the enclave and use the stipend to support earnings that she hoped to make from her writing. Or maybe she understood that an external pension constituted the first step toward winning the more desirable internal one in the not too distant future. But then again, perhaps she had requested a place in the enclave and had been given the external pension as a consolation prize.

Though it had obvious advantages, receiving a pension at the Quinze-Vingts would not guarantee Thérèse-Adèle an easy life in Paris. For one thing, it didn't provide her a place to live and full support for daily living. We know that material conditions were probably quite difficult because even after receiving the pension, Husson admitted regretting that she had given up the provincial life without obstacles—but also perhaps without joy—that she had shared with her family. According to her "Note on the Author's Youth" and the forewords of her other books, it seems that she rapidly found herself thrust into the Parisian maelstrom. Suddenly, she, who had always been sheltered from need and whose life had taken its course with "tranquillity" and "uniformity," nearly succumbed to poverty and indigence in the unforgiving city. Now the young girl from Nancy found herself alone in a hostile and dangerous place.

Again, however, we must be careful not to take all her descriptions at face value, at least when considering her early months in the capital. Much of what she says about her arrival in Paris corresponds to readers' expectations of what provincial newcomers were supposed to find there; in fact, it almost seems to mimic some of the popular novels about the provincial lost in Paris just as her later fiction seemed to imitate a particular kind of sentimental experience to follow the rules of that genre. To support this hypothesis, consider contradictory information from the archives. We know that a certain Nicolas Husson was among the witnesses whose signatures appear on the register of the parish Saint-Sulpice for her marriage to Pierre-François-Victor Foucault, on February 1, 1826.[57] None of Thérèse-Adèle's brothers were named Nicolas. He must have been an uncle or a cousin on her father's side; we don't know if he lived in Paris or if he journeyed to the capital only for the occasion. In either case, our traveler was probably less isolated than she would have liked the readers of her books to believe.

In addition to possible family connections, we know Husson looked to and received help from Parisian religious orders and from her association with the Quinze-Vingts, thanks to her benefactors in Nancy. The dedication of *Story of a Charitable Sister*, published in 1830, for example, shows that the Sisters of Saint Vincent de Paul were among the individuals who helped Thérèse-Adèle in her adventures. They could have found her a place to live and assisted her with setting up the household, bringing food and other necessities, guided her to various destinations, not to mention provided her with someone who could take dictation as she began her career as a writer. Besides religious people, not long after arriving in Paris the young woman met the man who would offer to share his life and his "limited resources" with her. We'd like to know more about the circumstances of how they met, since this would allow us to better understand how she lived and socialized apart from the nuns and the other kind people who helped her. Specifically, we wonder if the fact that she applied for a pension at the Quinze-Vingts introduced her into the social circles of the hospice's blind people and those of former students who had attended the Royal Institution for Blind Youth, all of whom had passed through the Quinze-Vingts because of the close ties between these institutions in the early years of the nineteenth century.

Indeed, her future husband, who was born on October 31, 1797, in Saint-Germain-le-Vieux-Corbeil, and who also had contracted smallpox in his early childhood, was raised at the school from 1806 to 1818. A booklet entitled "Listing of Students under the Care of the Royal Institution for Blind Youth of the Quinze-Vingts Imperial Hospice during 1813" notes that seven years after his arrival in the establishment, young Pierre-François-Victor was "quite successful in various fields of instruction."[58] Jean-François Galliod, a respected music teacher, described him as being among his "most distinguished students" in horn class, quite the compliment, since Dr. Sébastien Guillié, the institution's director and himself a good musician, had made music one of the cornerstones of the school's curriculum.[59] The institution's orchestra was led by a former student of Galliod's, Jean-Hippolyte Isman, who could still "see just a bit," enough to decipher scores, and who had an excellent reputation. Pierre-François-Victor Foucault would belong to this orchestra until his departure from the establishment. Zélie Cardeilhac, the head schoolmistress—a woman more likely to tout her own achievements than those of her pupils—cited him as being among its most accomplished members.[60]

Early on, Pierre-François-Victor showed other talents as well. One teacher commented on his "predisposition for mechanics," a trait that, as we'll soon learn, would make him famous much later in the small world of the blind.[61] He claimed distinction along with the school's other illustrious graduates. One, Jean-Baptiste Penjon, was a mathematician and married father of nine whose extraordinary talents made him the first blind person to be named professor in the French public school system and the first blind man to be awarded the Legion of Honor. The year after Pierre-François-Victor Foucault left the school, its most famous student of all, Louis Braille, entered. Here, when he was only in his teens, he would invent the system of tactile reading using cells of six raised dots still in use today. Interestingly, Braille chose not to draw attention to himself or his invention, and thus he remained relatively unknown outside blind circles until after his death in 1852. Successes by men such as these must have inspired future students while enhancing the school's national and international reputation.

Loosely attached to the Quinze-Vingts, the Royal Institution for Blind Youth had a rigid educational and disciplinary structure that reflected the era's quest to restore stability and morality in the wake of the French Revolution. Once the younger blind charges had been relocated to the decrepit buildings of the former seminary Saint-Firmin in 1815, new regulations from the Ministry of the Interior took effect that reduced the number of available spaces to 90, down from 120, so now the school allowed 60 boys and 30 girls. Its director, Dr. Guillié, had complete authority over the entire establishment and its occupants. As principal, he controlled all teachings, only having to report to the minister of the interior and the institution's administration, of which he was a member.

His ultimately controversial directorship would set an authoritarian tone.

Pierre-François-Victor's day was fifteen hours long, divided among intellectual work, music, manual chores, meals, leisure, and religious duties. Discipline was very strict while food was frugal; gender separation was total. To get some idea of how worried the school must have been about the morality of its charges, consider regulation 114:

> It is expressly forbidden for any student to raise a hand against anyone, and to commit any harmful action or any action contrary to morals and decency; all students found guilty of such infraction will be severely punished.[62]

Seven of the regulation's articles outlined punishments, while only five mentioned rewards. The most severe usually consisted of solitary confinement to the "discipline room" for one or several days, and, as a last resort, dismissal. A report on the institution's conditions shortly after Dr. Guillié's dismissal (allegedly for having had an affair with the head schoolmistress) described cruel and humiliating punishments:

> Two iron chains were and are still to be found, one in the dining hall, the other in the schoolyard; the boys were tied up and ignominiously punished like criminals; the younger like the older were so used to being whipped that they did not feel anything but the pain caused by this punishment. The executor, a man named Dominique, had died in Bicêtre not long ago

and was replaced by Simon, M. Guillié's servant. Girls were treated in the same manner, at a time in their lives when their health should have been even more respected. [. . .] Madame. . . , the water carrier, executed the most extreme punishments for a retribution of five sols.[63]

Such treatment was not unique to this school for the blind. In fact, had he been a sighted person, Pierre-François-Victor most likely would have had a similar experience in one of the mainstream schools beginning to be established at this time. The 1821 report regarding the Royal Institution for Blind Youth represented part of a growing movement to introduce more humanitarian treatment in schools throughout the country.[64]

However, another practice unique to the school continued, and it walked a fine line between seeking publicity for the school and exploiting the students' disabilities: putting pupils on public display to show off their expertise in various areas of knowledge. Guillié's *Report on the Institution's Conditions during 1818 and 1819* even boasts of how the room's capacity for spectators had increased to 400, up from 280 in previous years.[65] Popularized by the Abbé de l'Epée, the previous century's famous educator of deaf students, and soon afterwards by his counterpart for the blind, Valentin Haüy, this practice involved inviting the Parisian elites to observe pupils as they recited passages, played instruments, or solved mathematical equations. After Guillié's departure in 1821, an inspector affirmed that "these public exams were the goal of the teachings, and everything worked toward this single and ultimate end."[66] Administrators hoped that these displays of talent would show off their teaching successes and would encourage contributions from the wealthy. But surely, there must have also been a freak-show aspect that lured the spectators to come and watch the handicapped perform tricks as if in a circus. Because of his talents as a horn player, Pierre-François-Victor must have participated on a number of occasions.

An additional potential humiliation for the students involved Guillié's ambitions to link himself with the internationally acclaimed Paris medical community. Beginning in 1816, he took advantage of his role as the institution's chief physician to bring in colleagues to do free medical exams and attend public lectures on eye diseases. Soon after, he opened an eye clinic where, in 1819, he performed medical experiments on four blind youngsters to prove the contagious character of the disease purulent ophthalmia, publishing them in a medical magazine he had just founded called *Opthalmological Library, or A Collection of Observations on Eye Diseases.*[67] Such experiments, which were permitted on the poor who had entered hospitals for free, reveals the extent to which the distinction between "charity hospice" and "teaching establishment" remained blurred with regard to the Royal Institution for Blind Youth. They also demonstrate the abuse of power that could result from the confusion of duties of general director and of chief physician in an establishment that functioned as a boarding school mostly serving children from underprivileged families who lived far away. While their social standing might have made the poor more vulnerable to medical investigations, they also benefited from Guillié's willingness to operate on them for free, sometimes with favorable results. Because

of how the French medical community had been restruc-
tured in the aftermath of the Revolution, it would have
been difficult for someone like Guillié to have specialized
in ophthalmology until later in the century.[68]

Whatever Guillié's intentions, the institution he directed found itself in dire straits. The move in 1815 had
been costly, and little money could be found to repair the
decrepit buildings on the rue Saint-Victor. Later reports
by independent investigators criticized the institution's
sanitation and the poor health of numerous students
living there. (It's quite possible that Louis Braille contracted the tuberculosis that would lead to his early
death at the age of forty-three from these insalubrious
conditions.) But the environment wasn't the only problem. The public report also criticized the general quality
of education at the institution. After six years under
Guillié's ostentatious and despotic direction, investigators found the state of industrial education particularly
appalling. Having touted this program as one of the
great successes in the education of the blind, officials
now had to admit that some of the award-winning objects presented at the 1819 Exposition had not been
made by blind youth as they claimed, but had been
bought from outside manufacturers. Only musical and
religious teachings escaped without criticism.[69]

No doubt smarting from these revelations, the Ministry of the Interior hesitated to pour in the money
the Institution for Blind Youth would have needed to
survive, let alone thrive and serve the hundreds of people who needed it most. Despite a slight increase in
government funding between 1815 and 1825, by 1826
the institution's financial difficulties forced officials to

suspend students' nominations. Thus, the school that had served as a model for foreign countries, and where a system of reading had been invented that would forever open the lives of blind people to written culture, could no longer support and educate even the pathetically small number of blind students mandated by its charter.

Until the school got back on its feet several years later, young Foucault and his former classmates would have to rely largely on their own initiative to maintain the ongoing and vibrant blind community that surely helped Pierre-François-Victor and Thérèse-Adèle meet one another. We imagine them as part of a growing network of more intellectually inclined blind people drawn to the world of the Quinze-Vingts or the Royal Institution, even if they had been educated within their families or in a nonspecialized setting as Thérèse-Adèle Husson had been. Gathered together to share stories and ideas, they were beginning to develop a positive identity, possibly even one recognizable to the sighted world. They had their role models, such as old Pougens, the distinguished eighteenth-century linguist and translator respected beyond the world of blind people. But even from within their own class, individuals like Jean-Baptiste Penjon and Louis Braille began to emerge who would in turn set an example for those who followed.

Musicians like Foucault formed the most cohesive group coming from the Royal Institution. There was, for example, Claude Taboureau, a student of bass who later taught the instrument until 1814. He then left the school with four of his classmates (among them a female singer) to form the orchestra of a certain "Lafossé, café owner at Versailles," where they performed over the next two years.[70] Marie-Honorine-Stéphanie Flumser, Taboureau's wife, and Jean-Louis Bricard, a musician who lived at the Quinze-Vingts, were both close friends with Foucault.[71] Others included Pierre-Philippe Prévost, a former master flutist at the Royal Institution; Robert Labassé, a former master violinist also at the Institution; Jean-Hippolyte Isman, a flutist and the orchestra's conductor; and Charles Charaux, a violinist with much talent, who even incurred the wrath of a police official, who complained to the Royal Institution's director that Charaux was playing in disreputable locales.[72]

These blind musicians, some of whom played in the orchestra led by Galliod at the Quinze-Vingts, would also perform at the Café des Aveugles (Blind People's Café). Located in one of the basements of the Palais Royal, the club offered up entertainment by blind musicians in a shady quarter of Paris frequented by prostitutes, gamblers, and others of dubious distinction. Alternating with acts such as clown-like jugglers, a man known for dressing like a savage and dancing to wild drumbeats, and other carnivalesque entertainments, the orchestra of blind men (including several teachers and an occasional female singer) hovered on the edge of professional and moral respectability, much to the dismay of many administrators at the institutions for the blind.[73] Some contemporary writers described the locale as a "hideous den of rogues and prostitutes," with the Catholic ultra-royalists who ran the Quinze-Vingts looking particularly unfavorably upon their student-musicians or singers who performed in such immoral places at all hours.[74]

The Stage of the Café des Aveugles around 1800, Anonymous, Musée Carnavalet, D 3105.

A very different view of the Café des Aveugles. Anonymous cartoon, Musée Carnavalet, TOPO PC 033 D.

Indeed, a ban that the hospice had tried to place on these activities during the Restoration proved futile, and later under the July Monarchy the minister of the interior authorized blind musicians who resided at the Quinze-Vingts to play at night in cafés, "provided that they left half an hour before midnight" so as not to trouble "the order of the House" by returning at inappropriate hours.[75] Thus, from this day on, the profession of musician finally became an acceptable one for blind people, even when exercised outside religious institutions. Surely this helped broaden the numbers and scope of a cohesive blind community in Paris.

Whatever the circumstances of their meeting, young Thérèse-Adèle, living at number 53 rue des Boucheries, renounced her principles regarding blind women by marrying the poor blind musician Pierre-François-Victor Foucault on February 1, 1826.[76] Nicolas Husson, mentioned earlier, and a certain Jacques-Alexis Hérant served as Thérèse-Adèle's witnesses at the religious wedding, which took place in the Church of Saint-Sulpice in the parish where she lived. For the groom, Jean-Baptiste Robine, an uncle or first cousin on his mother's side, and a certain Alexandre-Julien Bardin signed the wedding certificate. Among the files of the Royal Institution for Blind Youth, we discovered that Bardin, the son of a disgraced schoolteacher, was Pierre-François-Victor's former classmate.[77] He knew how to sign his name, which is sufficiently legible for us to think he had some usable vision. However, "the spouses claimed not to know how to sign." While the wedding ceremony itself may have been short, we imagine that the musicians must have made for a lively party afterwards.

Marriage certificate of Pierre-François-Victor Foucault and Thérèse Husson, February 1, 1826. Register of Marriages, Parish of Saint-Sulpice, Archives de Paris/Archevêché, 1672.

Coming from a family far less prosperous than that of his new bride, the young Pierre-François-Victor had not had an easy life. From an unsuccessful petition that his mother made attempting to gain him a pension at the Quinze-Vingts when he was twenty-one, we know that Madame Foucault was a widow and the mother of three, including a girl with poor vision.[78] Due to a shortage of money, Pierre-François-Victor couldn't freely exercise the talents as a mechanic he had shown over the course of his twelve years of studies at the Royal Institution. Instead, he turned to his horn playing to earn a modest living by performing at the notorious Café des Aveugles. Somehow, the young Foucault managed to survive off his music, supplementing the little support he received from elsewhere with nights or afternoons in the jovial café.

Even if, as Thérèse-Adèle wrote in her "Note on the Author's Youth," Pierre-François-Victor managed to live off his meager earnings when he was single, their combined monthly incomes couldn't save them from poverty. The Quinze-Vingts archives contain traces of the couple's cries for help addressed to the hospice's administration between July 1828 and February 1830. These were years of a major European economic crisis, when cuts in salaries, unemployment, the escalating price of bread, and unusually hard winters took a particularly high toll on the Parisian lower classes. After having lived on the rue de Mézière near the Saint-Sulpice church in 1827, the couple moved to a much poorer neighborhood at 12 quai de Gèvres near the Hôtel de Ville (City Hall).[79] Populated by artisans, small shopkeepers, and some residents who had little or no money, the filthy and overcrowded area was singled out by city officials as one of the most unhealthy and dangerous in the entire capital. The 1828 *Almanach parisien* indicates that a tailor and another musician lived in their building, suggesting that perhaps the couple had found their new dwelling through Pierre-Francois-Victor's connections.[80] In a July 4, 1828, letter to the Grand Chaplain of France, Foucault requested an external pension from the hospice, citing his poor health, his "position as a father," and his job interruptions. Medical papers as well as certificates of poverty dated 1829 and 1830 indeed certify that he had been "suffering from a pulmonary catarrh for a number of years," and that in February 1830 the couple cared for a twenty-seven-month-old baby girl; indeed, records for the parish Saint-Sulpice listed the baptism of Stéphanie Pauline Nathalie Foucault on October 22, 1827.[81] Surely her birth added to the precariousness of the young couple's situation, which did not improve despite the publication of Husson's first novel, *The Converted Jewess*, at about the same time.

It's surprising that Husson couldn't have made more money from her pen, particularly since she had so much working in her favor. For one thing, she wrote in a genre that enjoyed much popular success at the same time that it endorsed the values of the regime in power. Establishing herself as a writer for young adults, she published novels and collections of short stories for children that continued a tradition of works with roots in the era before the French Revolution. For example, her collection *The Book of Moral Amusements, or Virtue in Action* took its title from a book by Laurent-Pierre Bérenger, a well-known work during the Restoration called *Morality in Action, or Chosen Memorable Facts and Instructive Anecdotes That*

Can Make Virtue Appealing and Train Young People in the Art of Narration, which had remained in print with multiple editions since 1783. The titles of Husson's other works followed this moralistic thread: *Eliza, or The Model of Filial Piety, Followed by The Unknown Benefactor, or Money's First Use* (1832); *The Three Sisters, or The Effects of Blind Motherhood* (a title that referred to blindness figuratively rather than literally) (1833); *The House in the Woods, or The Virtuous Family* (1836); *Recreational Evenings of a Country Priest* (1836); and finally, *Mélanie, or The Consequences of Ingratitude, Followed by The Young Blind Boys, or Memories of Illustrious Emigrants* (1838).[82] Published under the category of educational literature for young adults, these works constituted one of the few domains reserved almost exclusively for women writers.[83] Thus, our author's desperate struggle against poverty can't be blamed on her failure to write books that could sell.

Moreover, Husson seemed to be unusually well connected, a fact that helped ensure the publication and dissemination of her works. It's likely that in addition to providing spiritual guidance and helping her find a place to live, the religious community may have also played a role in putting the young provincial in touch with publishers and distributors of moral writings. As Husson put it, she drew the strength to send out her work from the encouraging words of "a few good and pious individuals." Such connections served an especially useful purpose, since the testimonies of numerous writers at the time revealed how difficult it was to publish, particularly for females. And the prospects for a young blind woman from the provinces living from her pen must have seemed even more impossible. Unfortunately, apart from the dedications to her books, we have no way of knowing exactly who helped her or what they did. We do know that based on her connections she succeeded in selling a few manuscripts—perhaps the very ones she listed at the end of her "Reflections"?—to bookstore-publishers, who, however, did not risk taking the costly step of putting them into print. Pressured by financial necessity, she probably sold them for a flat rate, following the example of several obscure women writers at the time. Such arrangements must have been a windfall for publishers if the unknown author ever became famous.[84]

Husson's writing benefited from these connections at the same time that it helped create them. We've already described how she had first asked for an external pension from the Quinze-Vingts after having addressed the manuscript of "Reflections" to La Croix d'Azolette. And as the dedications to her various books implied, she had built her literary career with the support of both throne and altar firmly in mind. For example, in the foreword to her *Book of Moral Amusements* she took pride in being able to cite, among numerous elite benefactors, "the good children of Saint-Louis [i.e., the Bourbons], comforting Angels who eased [her] sufferings and dried [her] tears!"[85] Protected by those who cared to bring France back to its "true" religion through the organization of Missions to the Interior, the propagation of "worthy books" [*les bons livres*], and the foundation of diverse institutions devoted to religiously charitable zeal, Husson-Foucault accepted—whether out of conviction or opportunism—to serve as a spokeswoman for antirevolutionary values embedded in the conservative Restoration. Indeed, as we've already noted, her first two novels,

The Converted Jewess and *Story of a Pious Heiress*, advocated that Jews and Protestants convert to Catholicism, calls echoed on a regular basis by ultraroyalist newspapers such as *L'Ami de la Religion et du Roi* and *La Quotidienne*. Less overtly strident, her other works were nevertheless grounded in the Catholic morals of her day, as their vocabulary makes clear. To quote the subtitle of one of her novels, *The Distinctive Orphan*, "piety, suffering, and courage" are three key words to which we can add others such as "resignation" (which she used often), and "expiation," so valued by the religious writers at the time. Such a moral tone would have captured the attention of potential Catholic supporters.

A good example of how Husson may have used her connections can be found in the specific case of her first published novel, *The Converted Jewess* (1827). It came out with a dedication to the Abbé Perreau, one of France's leading Catholics and, because of his stature, a high official at the Quinze-Vingts as well. Moreover, he played an important role as one of the directors of the Catholic Society for Worthy Books, an organization that most likely helped publicize and distribute her writings once they did make their way into print. Our savvy author thus had at least two good reasons to dedicate this first work to Abbé Perreau: not only did he have influence at the Quinze-Vingts, where she hoped to continue receiving financial support, but also he could help interest publishers in her work and arrange for its broad dissemination.

Clearly her strategy of courting the Abbé Perreau paid off. Though we found no mention of Husson-Foucault's books, it's possible that the Catholic Society for Worthy Books might have played an important role in making her work known to a broader public. First founded in the provinces at the beginning of 1824 and then introduced in Paris during July of the same year, the society had strong ties with the Quinze-Vingts. Its Parisian founder, the Duc Mathieu de Montmorency, served as one of the hospice's administrative governors and worked closely with the Abbé Perreau. This society had been created to fight the dissemination and influence of books "hostile to religion and contrary to morals."[86] It came at a time when book production and consumption expanded rapidly due to the development of primary school education, increasing literacy, and technical advances in the print industry.[87] Even though two years after its founding an impressive 800,000 volumes had already been distributed, the individuals promoting this society attempted to expand its audience even further by creating an association for making worthy books available free to the public. To this end, depositories opened not only in large cities but also in towns of all sizes. Striving to spread "all good doctrines, the love of God and of the King, the recognition of religion and the hatred of impiety," these centers sought to offset the enormous success of reading rooms that promoted less reputable titles.[88] The close connections between the society and the Quinze-Vingts where young Thérèse-Adèle first sought to make contacts in Paris suggest that her books thus may have been publicized with the help of the capital's most influential religious people.[89]

But how widely were Husson-Foucault's books distributed and how much money could she have earned from them? Even though we lack concrete evidence from her or from the Belin publishing house, we can offer some insights into her success as a writer in Restoration Paris. Thanks to Belin's catalogs kept in the Bibliothèque Nationale, for example, we know that the works of "Madame Foucault, born T. A. Husson" published while she was alive included *The Converted Jewess* (1827), *Story of a Pious Heiress* (1828), *The Book of Moral Amusements* (1829), and *Story of a Charitable Sister* (1830). They sold for three francs a copy and went into several printings, with *Story of a Pious Heiress* still appearing as late as 1849. From the registers of Parisian printers housed at the Archives Nationales, we also know that these first three novels each enjoyed print runs of between 1,500 and 2,000, respectable figures comparable to the numbers that a writer like George Sand would have a few years later.[90] Since Parisian publishing houses often sent their work out to be printed in the provinces, and since these small workshops didn't always keep detailed records, we unfortunately lack concrete data for her other books as well as for later editions. It's important to note, however, that the majority of her books appeared posthumously, so she didn't receive income from them. In any case, Madame Foucault was a successful author even if her occupation as a writer did not allow her to live decently.

Because of their occupations as writer and musician, it's difficult to classify Thérèse-Adèle and Pierre-François-Victor within the rigid social structure that characterized Paris during the Restoration. Indeed, on April 21, 1829, the Foucaults lived at 20 rue de Bourbon right in the middle of the fashionable Faubourg Saint Germain, a neighborhood where artisans, café owners, and people of letters mingled with dukes and princes. But we know this because the Tenth Arrondissement's[91] welfare rolls [*livre des pauvres*] listed the young couple among its neediest cases.[92] This gave them a right to material help, including the care of one Dr. Legras, who treated Pierre-François-Victor for chronic bronchitis and Thérèse-Adèle for a "nervous illness characterized by frequent crises of nerves" capable of "endangering her life." They were also registered for special assistance under the category of "blind persons," which allowed them to receive the modest sum of approximately six francs a month each in financial aid.[93]

Despite such help from the city, Thérèse-Adèle's external Quinze-Vingts pension, and the small income she received from the sale of her books (the first two were republished at this time), the couple's situation grew even more critical in February 1830, when she expected another child.[94] On May 24 she gave birth to a second girl, Marie Geneviève Elisa.[95] In August, probably pressured by difficulties in paying rent or by the need for more space after the addition of a new child, the young parents moved again, this time to the rue de Sartine in the more squalid Fourth Arrondissement. Once again, they joined the welfare rolls and signed up for special assistance under the category of "blind persons."[96] And once again, they turned to the Quinze-Vingts.

Even though they had managed to convince various city offices in different neighborhoods of their desperate need for help, the couple failed to win over the hospice's administrators. To be sure, since the many requests for places in the enclave far exceeded the number of available spaces and pensions, it was difficult to obtain a favorable answer, even with a respectable dossier or with recommendations from powerful individuals. It seems, however, that the Foucaults' failure might have had another cause. Interestingly, their first letter to the Grand Chaplain, dated July 4, 1828, had two notes scrawled in its margins. The first, signed "✝ Charles, Bishop of Nancy and of Toul" is a recommendation from Monseigneur de Forbin-Janson, a pillar of the Restoration, in favor of the petitioners. The second, in La Croix d'Azolette's handwriting, indicates that "The Director [of the Institution] for Blind Youth" had expressed "some serious complaints regarding the moral values of this couple" to his counterpart at the Quinze-Vingts. "Above all," La Croix d'Azolette continues, "he says that the woman is a schemer who has taken advantage of several individuals [*la femme est une intrigante qui a trompé la bonne foi de plusieurs personnes*]. . . . There have also been complaints regarding their morals, etc. . . . Monseigneur de Nancy would also have been deceived."[97] Such unfavorable commentary surely dashed the young couple's hopes, though maybe only temporarily, if the power of Thérèse-Adèle's protectors like the exalted Forbin-Janson could perhaps convince his colleagues to change their minds. Unfortunately for the struggling family, officials refused twice, in 1829 and in 1830, thus making the decision final.

Thérèse-Adèle Husson-Foucault died tragically on March 30, 1831, at six A.M. at the Hôtel-Dieu from what the hospital's records described as "burns" that probably covered much of her body. She was only twenty-eight years old. Five weeks earlier, the couple had been admitted after fire consumed their apartment, probably when flames escaped from the tiny stove they would have used for cooking and heating.[98] Unfortunately, we couldn't

A letter from Pierre-François-Victor Foucault to the Cardinal Prince of Croÿ, July 4, 1828. Administrative file of Madame Foucault (Thérèse-Adèle) born Husson, Archives of the Quinze-Vingts, P48 3506. Marginal notes comment on the morality of the household.

track down any police or fire department reports to clar-
ify the circumstances of the accident. We can only imagine that her death was long and excruciatingly painful,
since medical science had not yet developed antibiotics,
sterilized wound dressings, nutritional therapies, or ef-
fective surgical and graft techniques for burns, let alone
the potent painkillers that we take for granted today.
And even if some remedies had existed, they weren't
likely to be found at the Hôtel-Dieu or any other hospital in the first half of the nineteenth century. Though at
this time Paris was widely heralded as the medical capital
of the world, hospitals remained much the same as they
had been during their founding in the Middle Ages: religiously run institutions that served as repositories of
desperate poor and disabled people. In fact, their filth,
lack of sterilization, scampering rats, drafty, dark wards,
and dangerous overcrowding, along with untrained and
overworked employees, meant that Husson could just
as easily have died from disease or other complica-
tions. Moreover, it's more than likely that she suffered
through her final weeks while sharing her bed with at
least one other patient, a common practice in early-nine-
teenth-century hospitals. It's no wonder that the wealthy
spurned these warehouses of the hopeless urban poor to
be treated at home. That Thérèse-Adèle died so miserably
in such a place says just how desperate her circumstances
had become, even as she had reached the height of her
professional success.

Pierre-François-Victor, on the other hand, survived
the ordeal, going on to become an inventor with a
modest national reputation. Nearly two years after the
fire he married a seamstress, Adèlaïde-Louise Juteau.[99]

Apparently, they had no children, and the historical record leaves no traces of the two daughters he had had with Thérèse-Adèle. Did they live with their parents before their mother's death, or had they already been left in the care of someone else such as a wet nurse, a common practice for poor people at the time? Or were they present the day of the accident? Could they have died immediately in the fire or on the way to the hospital? Or perhaps, like so many other children from all classes at the time, the girls had died earlier from some infantile illness? In any case, they don't appear on the admission records of the Hôtel-Dieu, nor did we find any other documents that mentioned them. Not even the registries for the Third and Fourth Arrondissements that recorded Thérèse-Adèle's death listed the daughters as heirs. Most tellingly, when Pierre-François-Victor made another appeal to enter the Quinze-Vingts as a resident pensioner in the year before he remarried, he didn't invoke his role as a father to win sympathy.

We'll never know if help from the Quinze-Vingts would have prolonged Thérèse-Adèle's life. With it, the Foucault family might have been able to afford rent on an apartment less vulnerable to human carelessness. Perhaps more money would have freed the young mother of two from her "crises of nerves" and other pressures before it was too late.

It's worth following Pierre-François-Victor a few decades into the future in order to get some perspective on how Thérèse-Adèle might have been responsible for the family's desperate circumstances. Tellingly, after her death, the Quinze-Vingts admitted him as a "blind member" on January 25, 1832, with him entering as a resident just under two weeks later on February 8.[100] We know that his new wife was sighted, since there seemed to be no problem with her joining him in the enclave. Sighted people often drifted into the hospice's orbit in search of romance or financial rewards. Some, of course, tried to take advantage, but for many it seemed to promise a secure life beyond their dreams, a refuge from the hardships of the precarious city life. As a result, vigilant administrators constantly fretted not just over possible moral trans-gressions, but also over the likelihood that many newcomers might steal or otherwise abuse the residents. We'll never know if the young seamstress who worked as a laundress came to her new marriage for love or money or some combination of the two, just as we'll remain ignorant of what kind of marriage Thérèse-Adèle enjoyed with Pierre-François-Victor in their five years together. We know for certain, however, that life grew much easier for Monsieur Foucault in his second marriage.

Admitted to the Quinze-Vingts less than a year after the death of his blind spouse, and later authorized to remarry Mademoiselle Juteau, Pierre-François-Victor was soon able "to be more at ease financially" by managing a small grocery store on the hospital grounds. The store's income could be added to what he earned as a musician at the Café des Aveugles and his stipend as a boarder at the hospice. Thus, he could give free rein to his imagination in the realm of mechanics and become useful to his "brothers in misfortune" by inventing a mechanism that allowed blind people to correspond with sighted readers. Called a "raphigraph," it mechanically created conventional print letters according to Louis Braille's system, which enabled blind people to communicate with those who read print. Foucault put it to the test at the Quinze-Vingts using his blind musician friends from the Café des Aveugles. After receiving a medal in 1843 from the Society for the Encouragement of National Industry and later one at the 1851 Universal Exposition held in London, this product of Foucault's genius and of his collaboration with other educated blind men was used for about forty years among French blind people.[101] It was also sold abroad, especially in schools for the blind that had been founded on the French model in many countries across Europe and in the United States. Even though there would be no way of proving it, we can't help but wonder if Pierre-François-Victor's inspiration came in part from the memory of the difficulties that his first wife encountered as she was obliged to use the services of scribes in order to continue her work as a professional writer. Pierre-François-Victor died forty years after his first wife, in 1871.

In light of Foucault's longevity and his later professional success, we must consider the fact that Thérèse-Adèle played an important role in her family's demise, even if it wasn't necessarily her fault. The key to understanding this tragedy lies in the Quinze-Vingts' ultimately devastating refusal of the couple's petition, despite how closely she seemed to adhere to the most important values of her day and how well-placed her supporters seemed to be. Why would someone like La Croix d'Azolette turn on her and proclaim her a "schemer" when her publishing career in edifying moralistic fiction seemed to be reaching its heights of success and influence? To be sure, the young writer from the provinces defied many social taboos both as a woman and as a blind individual, not to mention as a blind woman.

The fact that Thérèse-Adèle married a blind man surely played a part. We already know that she understood the social consequences of breaking the taboo because she condemned the practice in her "Reflections," written in part to curry favor with the moralistic Quinze-Vingts administrators. However, she probably wasn't aware of the reasons behind the explicit prohibition, rooted in laws that went back to the institution's founding six centuries earlier. Ironically, the hospital's regulations mentioned "fear of fire" as a reason for forbidding households that consisted only of blind individuals. These concerns of Michel de Brache, chaplain to King Jean II Le Bon from 1351 to 1355, stayed on administrators' minds long after they disappeared from the official regulations. And not only did officials argue that unsupervised blind people posed a danger to themselves and others, they also believed them incapable of living independently. Sighted spouses of pensioners could render useful services to both their partners and the institution as a whole. They could of course help with household chores, run errands beyond the enclave, or possibly bring in a better income than the average blind person. But they could also serve policing functions as the eyes and ears of the administration in an environment wary of moral transgressions that might occur between residents dependent on their sense of touch. Even if officials feared that sighted people entered the enclave for less than upstanding reasons, it seemed that they felt more comfortable with a certain number of them around.

In addition to challenging the long-standing rules against marrying a blind man, Thérèse-Adèle may have alienated her protectors for political reasons. Even though the Restoration Bourbon monarchy and the Catholic Church were firmly entrenched by the time the young provincial woman arrived in Paris, she might have unknowingly found herself in the midst of internal conflicts and power struggles that plague every administration. The couple may have been victims of a rivalry dividing the Catholic elite at the time. It would be easy for an official on the defensive to accuse a young woman who showed any audacity of being a "schemer" simply because she had carelessly sought the support of someone who belonged to the wrong faction. Moreover, it's conceivable that the resounding victory of the Orleanist July Monarchy after the 1830 revolution ensured that Pierre-François-Victor—spurned by the previous enemy Bourbons—would more easily receive a coveted place in a hospital run by a new administration the year after his first wife's death.

And even if she hadn't accidentally found herself on the wrong side of some small or large-scale political conflict, Madame Foucault may have alienated someone by living a private life that blatantly contradicted so many of the morals she espoused in print. Surely, as a musician and a writer, the Foucaults fell under suspicion. Restoration officials had been wary of artists because they seemed to link independent creative activity and immorality, the Foucaults being no exception. Remember that Pierre-François-Victor played his horn in the disreputable Café des Aveugles and kept company with musicians who freely indulged in performing nonreligious

music. At the same time, Thérèse-Adèle degraded wom-
ankind by—like her sisters of letters—living a public life
as a writer. As late as 1866, the religious figure Monseigneur Dupanloup would advise women not to embark
on a literary career except "on condition that they write
only for their children, and they never be published," an
indication of just how strong these ideas must have been
during Husson's time.[102] Obviously, the young author
broke most of his rules.

Thus, while her moralistic, religiously righteous protectors may have guaranteed Husson's literary success,
she might have been more careful to conform to their
expectations of her behavior as a blind woman from
the provinces. She negotiated contracts and published
books, married a blind man, and probably had a forceful
personality, all things that would have raised serious
concerns for her supporters. And what might alienate
one's friends could be lethal in the hands of one's enemies. The seemingly insignificant faux pas in one's private life, imprudence in one's choice of associates, the
slightest strategic mistake when seeking more support,
not to mention the slightest slander, might each provide
the excuse for a humiliating attack on both the perpetra-
tor and those associated with her. It's precisely during
such moments that one can be accused of being an op-
portunist, or worse, of being immoral. Ironically, we
know that Husson understood this all too well because
she stated as much in her "Reflections" as well as in her
subsequent writings. Alas, by not following her own advice, young Thérèse-Adèle Husson lived out many of the
terrifying predictions she had made, including the circumstances of her own early and tragic death.

Finally, it's possible that Thérèse-Adèle Husson may have alienated her benefactors not just because of her behavior as a woman but also because of what she tried to accomplish as a blind person. To be sure, she did not fit the popular image of blind people trotted out in literature, etchings, drama, and songs that made blindness so widely discussed in the eighteenth and early nineteenth centuries. Though many different—and sometimes even contradictory—representations existed, certain commonalities suggested that the public had definite ideas, at least as far as popular entertainment was concerned. For example, one sentimental ballad from 1827 printed in *Troubadour des Salons* with text and music by Charles Malo was called "Pity the Poor Blind," a song that promoters guaranteed would "soon be played on every piano in the capital."[103] In drama blindness brought in money, whether the effects were moving or comic. The runaway success of Scribe and Mélesville's 1822 sentimental comedy called *Valérie*—whose heroine recovers her sight thanks to surgery performed on her by the man whom she loves (and who learns the art of surgery for her benefit)—was followed by numerous knockoffs, including a case of outright plagiarism and several spoofs.[104] Drawings of lone blind beggars with their dogs, miraculous stories of mistaken identity and regained sight, and stories of wandering blind orphans all contributed to making blindness simultaneously terrifying and exotic.

Of course we suspect that Thérèse-Adèle's editor— with her own complicity—counted on the public's interest when he mentioned Madame Foucault's blindness on the title pages of her novels, just as other respected writers did.[105] But this doesn't mean that some of the popular representations and even the interest itself were not at times painful. When all was said and done, the public imagination was limited with respect to blindness; one could be a beggar and a grateful recipient of charity or one could be a miracle as the result of restored vision. Learning to meet these expectations while still being true to herself and her dreams was perhaps Thérèse-Adèle Husson's biggest challenge of all, and maybe the one that ultimately cost her her life.

Perhaps, then, Husson posed a threat to her protectors because she didn't fulfill their expectations of a blind person. For one thing, with the success of her books and her public presence as a woman writer, she might have become a less attractive charity case in the eyes of her noble protectors. Even though she obviously still needed assistance, she had a career that displayed a streak of independence and an ability for taking the initiative that many would have found unattractive, even threatening in a poor blind girl from the provinces. Charity was largely about establishing a power relationship between the donor and recipient in the hopes of preserving the status quo. After all, most of the nobles and Church officials who would have come to Husson's aid owed their positions to French society being the way it was. As a result, they helped the blind not because they wanted to change the structures that kept the unfortunates in a state of dependency or because they hoped to improve society's unfavorable picture of them, but because they got something out of it themselves. Whether motivated out of guilt, fear, lofty Christian sentiment, or genuine concern, most of Husson's benefactors expected that their contribution would enhance their own situation without actually changing the world that had given them power. If someone went against the grain, it might be tantamount to being ungrateful for charity. While Thérèse-Adèle may have rewarded some of her protectors' impulses by prostrating herself in her prose, her personal life suggested that she was less beholden to her benefactors after all.

Moreover, Thérèse-Adèle and her husband challenged a powerful yet never openly stated social taboo by mingling with other blind people, even seeking out their company to form a support network beyond the reach of an institution. To be sure, in her "Reflections" Husson expressly stated that she had "always taken a certain pleasure in seeking out the company of other blind people," while the very existence of this manuscript in which she addresses "her comrades of misfortune" indicates that she wanted to bring them together. Until the second half of the twentieth century, however, there were few, if any, popular depictions of such positive bonding taking place. In many representations blind people, like their comrades in most other disabilities (with the exception of deaf people), only appear as isolated individuals left to navigate the world's troubled waters with the help of sighted guides. Seldom did the sighted world depict them positively as they congregated together, even though we know that groups such as musicians formed lively networks of association. Not until the twentieth century do we have examples of blind people collectively challenging what the broader society thought of them. Thus, when the Foucaults gathered together with the musicians at the Café des Aveugles, the threat to the status quo may not have been limited to questions of morality. Of course, since other musicians had entered the Quinze-Vingts without encountering resistance, officials didn't appear to object to their profession, thus suggesting that the Foucaults hadn't been denied for this reason. Even so, it's worth considering the impact that such associations might have had on the minds of administrators. Still reeling from a revolution that had unleashed calls for human rights on behalf of other marginal groups such as the poor, women, and people of different races, these anxious men of the Restoration might well have viewed a woman whose "Reflections" had explicitly addressed other blind people as a provocateur, an instigator of dangerous ideas.

When all is said and done, we lack the smoking gun that would solve the mystery of Husson's fall from grace. We can only acknowledge how difficult it must have been for poor blind people—however educated or enterprising—to live off their work and to escape the control that individuals running public assistance services like the Quinze-Vingts exercised over them. Desperate and afraid, most blind people accepted these conditions, quietly living out their lives without asking too much. Among them, however, was Thérèse-Adèle Husson, whose desire to be socially recognized, whose audacity to write with the voice of an expert, and whose dreams of happiness cost her the most. As short and difficult as her life was, she at least lived it fully and with the dignity of someone who had dared to speak her mind.

NOTES

Notes to the Introduction

1. See, for example, Dr. Emile Javal, *Entre aveugles: Conseils à l'usage des personnes qui viennent de perdre la vue* (Paris, 1903); Maurice de la Sizeranne, *Les Aveugles par un aveugle* (Paris, 1890); Pierre Villey, *Le Monde des aveugles* (Paris, 1914); William Henry Gregg, *Secrets of Fate Unlocked: From Possibility to Reality* (n.p., 1901).

2. Zina Weygand, "La Cécité et les aveugles dans la société française: Réprésentations et institutions du Moyen Age aux premières années du XIXe siècle," Thèse pour le Nouveau Doctorat, Université Paris I, 1998.

3. Dr. Georges Dumont, *Recherches statistiques sur les causes et les effets de la cécité* (Paris: Labé, 1856), 8; Ordonnance du 3 juillet 1945 sur la protection sociale des infirmes et incurables.

4. Charles Pougens, *Mémoires et souvenirs de Charles Pougens, commencés par lui et continués par Mme Louise B. de Saint-Léon* (Paris: Librairie de H. Fournier Jeune, 1834).

5. *Trésor des origines, ou Dictionnaire grammatical raisonné de la langue française* (Paris, 1819).

6. Jean-Charles-François, Baron de Ladoucette, *Notice sur M. le chevalier de Pougens* (n.p., n.d.), 3.

7. "Réflections sur l'état physique et moral des aveugles par Mlle Adelle Husson, jeune aveugle de Nanci," [1825], MS Archives des Quinze-Vingts, B115/5858.

8. Madame Foucault, née T. A. Husson, *Histoire d'une pieuse héritière, ou L'Heureux résultat de la confiance en Dieu*, 4th ed. (Paris: Belin–Le Prieur, 1836), "Notice sur la jeunesse de l'auteur."

Note to *Reflections on the Physical and Moral Condition of the Blind*

Bracketed ellipses indicate additions made by us; unbracketed ellipses are according to Husson's original text.

Notes to *Reflections on a Manuscript, a Life, and a World*

1. We use "Thérèse-Adèle Husson" in our discussion, even though she used numerous variations throughout her life. For example, she wrote the "Réflections" as "Adèle Husson," whereas other works appeared under "Thérèse-Adèle Husson" or "T. A. Husson," or later, after her marriage, "Madame Foucault." Her birth certificate lists her as "Thérèse Husson," while this single name also appeared on various official documents.

2. *Lettre sur les aveugles à l'usage pour ceux qui voient* (London, 1749).

3. Zina Weygand, "La Lettre (1749) et ses Additions (1782): La parole aux aveugles," *Voir Barré: Périodique du Centre de recherche sur les aspects culturels de la vision* 18 (May 1999), 16–29.

4. Mark Traugott, ed., *The French Worker: Autobiographies from the Early Industrial Era* (Berkeley: University of California Press, 1993); Alfred Kelly, ed., *The German Worker: Working-Class Autobiographies from the Age of Industrialization* (Berkeley: University of California Press, 1987).

5. Alexandre Rodenbach, *Lettre sur les aveugles faisant suite à celle de Diderot, ou Considérations sur leur état moral, comment on les*

instruit, comment ils jugent des couleurs, de la beauté, ainsi que leur méthode pour converser avec les sourds-muets, suivies de notices biographiques sur les aveugles les plus remarquables (Brussels: Imprimerie de J. Sacré, 1828).

6. Rebecca Rogers, "Competing Visions of Girls' Secondary Education in Post-Revolutionary France," *History of Education Quarterly* 34, no. 2 (summer 1994): 147–70; Françoise Mayeur, *L'Éducation des filles en France au XIXe siècle* (Paris: Hachette, 1979).

7. Dr. Sébastien Guillié, *Essai sur l'instruction des aveugles, ou Exposé analytique des procédés employés pour les instruire* (1817; Paris, 1819).

8. "Considérations générales sur l'esprit et le caractère des aveugles."

9. Mayeur, *Education des filles*, 47.

10. Comtesse Dash, *Le Livre des femmes* (Paris, 1860), cited in Michelle Perrot, "De la vieille fille à la garçonne: La femme célibataire au XIXe siècle," *Autrement* 32 (May 1981): 222.

11. Madame de Rémusat, *Essai sur l'éducation des femmes, précédé d'une étude par Octave Gréard* (1824; Paris: Librairie Hachette et Cie, 1903), 74; Cecilia de Luna Folliero, *De l'éducation des femmes, ou Moyens de les faire contribuer à la félicité publique, en assurant leur propre bien-être* (Paris: Ambroise Dupont), cited in the *Journal des Dames et des Modes* 45 (August 1827): 359; Rémusat, *Essai sur l'éducation*, 4.

12. Madame F. Mongellaz, *De l'influence des femmes sur les mœurs et les destinées des nations, sur leurs familles et la société, et de l'influence des mœurs sur le bonheur de la vie* (Paris: L.-G. Michaud, 1828).

13. Ibid., cited in the *Journal des Dames et des Modes* 54 (September 1828): 429–30.

14. Catherine J. Kudlick, "The Helpless and the Hopeless in Cross-Cultural Context: Images of Blindness and Gender Stereotypes in Late Nineteenth-Century France and America"

(paper presented at Berkshire Conference of Women Historians, Rochester, New York, June 1999).

15. *La Juive convertie, ou Le Triomphe du christianisme, suivi de L'Orpheline de distinction, ou Piété, malheur et courage* (1827), *Le Passe-temps moral, ou La Vértu mise en action* (1829), and *Histoire d'une soeur de charité* (1830).

16. Martyn Lyons, *Le Triomphe du livre: Une histoire sociologique de la lecture dans la France du XIXe siècle* (n.p.: Promodis, Editions du Cercle de la Librairie, 1987).

17. *Les Trois soeurs, ou Les Effets de l'aveuglement maternel* (Paris, 1833); and *Mélanie, ou Les Suites de l'ingratitude, suivi des Deux aveugles, ou Souvenirs d'illustres émigrés* (1838).

18. *Histoire d'une soeur*, 58–59.

19. To re-create the lives of Thérèse-Adèle, her family, and her eventual husband, we researched in the following archives and libraries (all in Paris unless otherwise specified): the Quinze-Vingts Hospital, particularly the dossiers concerning pensioners in the hospice during the Restoration and the July Monarchy; the Institut National des Jeunes Aveugles; the Archives Nationales; Archives Municipales de Nancy; Archives Départementales de l'Essonne; the Archives de Paris et du Département de la Seine; the Archives de l'Assistance Publique—Hôpitaux de Paris, the Association Valentin Haüy, and the Bibliothèque Nationale de France.

20. Stendhal wrote the novel between 1834 and 1836, but it was only published in 1894.

21. From René Taveneaux, *Histoire de Nancy* (Toulouse: Privat, 1978).

22. L'épiscopat Français, *Depuis le Concordat jusqu'à la Séparation 1802–1905,* vol. 1 (Paris: Librairie des Saints-Pères, 1907), 384.

23. Ibid.

24. Christian Pfister, *Histoire de Nancy,* vol. 3 (Paris, Nancy: Berger-Levrault et Cie, 1908–09), 324.

25. Taveneaux, *Histoire de Nancy,* 330.

26. Sheryl Kroen, *Politics and Theater: The Crisis of Legitimacy in Restoration France, 1815–1830* (Berkeley: University of California Press, 2000), 76–108; Ernest Sevrin, *Les Missions religieuses en France sous la Restauration,* 2 vols. (Paris: Librairie Philosophique J. Vrin, 1959).

27. "Registre de population, année 1807, 4e section," MS Archives Municipales de Nancy.

28. "Acte de décès de Marc Husson, du 2 octobre 1808," MS Archives Municipales de Nancy.

29. Paroisse Saint-Pierre, "Mariage de Marc Husson et Anne Millot, le 24 avril 1787," MS Archives Municipales de Nancy, Mi.27.GG.134.

30. "Acte de mariage de Joseph Martin, veuf de Jeanne Dupuy, et d'Anne Millot, veuve de Marc Husson, Mairie de Nancy, le 3 août 1809," MS Archives Municipales de Nancy.

31. "Registre de population, année 1820, 2e section," MS Archives Municipales de Nancy.

32. See *Les Trois soeurs.*

33. Zina Weygand, *Les Causes de la cécité et les soins oculaires en France au début du XIXe siècle (1800–1815)* (Paris: C.T.N.E.R.H.I., 1989), 95–118; Yves-Marie Bercé, *Le Chaudron et la lancette: Croyances populaires et médecine préventive, 1798–1830* (Paris: Presses de la Renaissance 1984), 63–98.

34. Pfister, *Histoire de Nancy,* vol. 2, 1022.

35. Abbé Girard, *La Charité à Nancy* (Nancy: Pierron et Hozé, 1890), 89.

36. Pfister, *Histoire de Nancy,* vol. 2, 732.

37. Etienne Thévenin, "L'Institution des Jeunes Aveugles de Nancy de sa fondation (1852) à 1914," *Les Annales de l'Est* (January 1997): 99–130.

38. Quoted in Isabelle Bricard, *Saintes ou pouliches: L'éducation des jeunes filles au XIXe siècle* (Paris: Albin Michel, 1985), 46.

39. Quoted in Bricard, *Saintes ou pouliches,* 50.

40. Quoted in ibid., 52.

41. *Economie politique chrétienne, ou Recherches sur la nature et les causes du paupérisme en France et en Europe*, 3 vols. (Paris, 1834).

42. Evelyne Lejeune-Resnick, "Les Femmes écrivains sous la Monarchie de Juillet (Société et littérature)" (diss., University of Paris IV, n.d.), 64–65.

43. Alain Corbin, seminar, "Un Exemple de représentations de l'espace: La Province selon Balzac et selon Stendhal," University of Paris I, 1999.

44. Ministère de l'Intérieur, "Du 23 ventôse an IX, Réglements pour l'organisation de cet hospice, chapitre 2: Nombre, secours, et régime des aveugles," MS Archives Quinze-Vingts, B106/6610.

45. Hôpital Royal des Quinze-Vingts. "Registre des délibérations de l'administration dudit Hôpital, du 16 juillet 1819 au 20 janvier 1824, Séance du 1er décembre 1823," MS Archives des Quinze-Vingts.

46. "Premier rapport confidentiel du Chevalier de La Croix d'Azolette au Grand Aumônier sur l'administration des Quinze-Vingts, 30 juin 1824," MS Archives des Quinze-Vingts, B107/6685.

47. "Registre destiné à recueillir les délibérations et arrêtés de l'administration des Quinze-Vingts, par notre administrateur provisoire de cet hospice [Cochin], du 5 septembre 1831 au 24 juin 1835; 14 novembre 1832," MS Archives des Quinze-Vingts.

48. Hôpital Royal des Quinze-Vingts, "Registre des délibérations de l'administration dudit Hôpital, du 31 juillet 1824 au 6 décembre 1826, Séance du 21 février 1825, Arrêté de l'administration sur le pain, le vêtement et les secours, article 5," MS Archives des Quinze-Vingts.

49. Ibid. Séance du 10 janvier 1825.

50. "Premier Rapport confidentiel du Chevalier de La Croix d'Azolette."

51. Léon Le Grand, *Les Quinze-Vingts depuis leur fondation jusqu'à leur translation au faubourg St. Antoine, 13e–18e siècle* (Paris, 1887).

52. Hôpital Royal des Quinze-Vingts, "Registre des délibérations. Du 31 juillet 1824 au 6 décembre 1826, Séance du 28 février 1825, Tableau des divers arts et métiers exercés par les habitans de la Maison," MS Archives des Quinze-Vingts.

53. Catherine J. Kudlick, *Cholera in Post-Revolutionary Paris: A Cultural History* (Berkeley: University of California Press, 1996), chap. 1.

54. "Recherches statistiques," quoted in Louis Chevalier, *Laboring Classes and Dangerous Classes in Paris during the First Half of the Nineteenth Century*, English trans. (Princeton: Princeton University Press, 1973), 187.

55. Hospice des Quinze-Vingts, "Enregistrement des aveugles aspirants, Registre n° 2, à compter du 1er janvier 1811 depuis le n° 1748 jusques et y compris le n° 3111 (27 décembre 1830), N° 2651, 25 mars 1825," MS Archives des Quinze-Vingts.

56. Grande Aumônerie, "Affaires diverses, recommandations, etc. . . . 1814–1830," MS Archives Nationales, O/3/18.

57. "Mariage de Pierre-François-Victor Foucault et Thérèse Husson, le 1er février 1826, Paroisse Saint-Sulpice, Registre des mariages, 1826," MS Archives de Paris/Archevêché, 1672.

58. "Tableau des élèves entretenus dans l'Institution des Jeunes Aveugles de l'Hospice Impérial des 15-20, pendant l'Exercice 1813," MS Archives Nationales, F15/2575.

59. Jean-François Galliod, "Note sur l'Etablissement des Jeunes Aveugles réunis aux Quinze-Vingts en 1801, adressée à M. Haüy, à son retour en France, par M. Galliod son ancien élève, maître de musique des Quinze-Vingts," *Liste de mes élèves qui se sont le plus distingués* (n.d. [1817]), 8, MS Archives Institut National des Jeunes Aveugles de Paris.

60. Zélie Lagrange-Cardeilhac, "Lettre à Joseph Guadet en

réponse à sa publication sur l'Institution des Aveugles, Paris, 15 juillet 1861," MS Bibliothèque Valentin Haüy, Archives Maurice de La Sizeranne.

61. Joseph Guadet, "Les aveugles mécaniciens," *Annales de l'Éducation des Sourds-Muets et des Aveugles* 2 (1844–5): 233.

62. "Réglement pour l'Institution Royale des Jeunes Aveugles, arrêté le 18 octobre 1815, article 114," MS Archives Institut National des Jeunes Aveugles de Paris.

63. Dr. Pignier, "Rapport fait au Conseil d'administration de l'Institution Royale des Jeunes Aveugles par le directeur de l'établissement, du 19 mai 1821," MS Archives Institut National des Jeunes Aveugles de Paris.

64. Jean-Claude Caron, *A l'école de la violence: Châtiments et sévices dans l'institution scolaire au XIXe siècle* (Paris: Aubier, 1999).

65. Dr. Guillié, *Rapport fait à Son Excellence le Ministre, Secrétaire d'état au département de l'Intérieur, par M. Guillié, sur l'état de l'Institution Royale des Jeunes Aveugles pendant les exercices 1818 et 1819* (Paris: de l'Imprimerie de J.-L. Chanson, Imprimeur de l'Institution, 1820), 8.

66. *Rapport de M. Letronne,* in Pignier, "Rapport fait au Conseil d'administration de l'Institution Royale des Jeunes Aveugles.

67. *La Bibliothèque Ophtalmologique, ou Recueil d'Observation sur les Maladies des Yeux.*

68. The law of March 13, 1803, eliminated specializations such as ophthalmology. Weygand, *Les Causes de la cécité*, 35.

69. *Rapport de M. Letronne.*

70. Galliod, "Note sur l'Établissement des Jeunes Aveugles."

71. Flumser would become the godmother to the Foucaults' eldest daughter, while Bricard would become godfather to their youngest. "Baptême de Stéphanie Pauline Nathalie [Foucault], le mardi 23 octobre 1827, Paroisse Saint-Sulpice, Registre des baptêmes 1827 et 1828," MS Archives de Paris/Archevêché, 3678; "Baptême de Marie Geneviève Elisa [Foucault], le samedi

29 mai 1830, Paroisse Saint-Thomas d'Aquin, Registre des baptêmes de l'année 1830," MS Archives de Paris/Archevêché, 3723.

72. "Lettre du Directeur de la Police à M. le Directeur de l'Institution des Jeunes Aveugles, Paris, le 20 novembre 1822, Signée: Franchet Desperey," MS Archives Institut National des Jeunes Aveugles de Paris.

73. Guillaume de Bertier de Sauvigny, *Nouvelle histoire de Paris: La Restauration 1815–1830* (Paris: diffusion Hachette, 1997), 380.

74. Auguste Luchet, *Paris, Esquisses dédiées au peuple parisien . . .* (Paris, 1830), 271, cited in Bertier de Sauvigny, *Nouvelle histoire de Paris: La Restauration 1815–1830,* 380; "Premier rapport confidentiel du Chevalier de La Croix d'Azolette."

75. "Registre destiné à recueillir les délibérations et arrêtés de l'administration des Quinze-Vingts, par notre administrateur provisoire de cet hospice [Cochin], du 5 septembre 1831 au 24 juin 1835; 18 novembre [1831]," MS Archives des Quinze-Vingts.

76. "Mariage de Pierre-François-Victor Foucault et Thérèse Husson."

77. "Dossiers personnels d'Alexandre-Julien Bardin," MS Archives des Quinze-Vingts, P39/2416, and MS Archives Nationales, F15/2575 and F15/2583.

78. "Pétition de la veuve Foucaud à Son Eminence Monseigneur le Cardinal Grand Aumônier de France, le 10 décembre 1818, Dossier Foucault (ou Foucaud)," MS Archives des Quinze-Vingts, P48/3507.

79. "Baptême de Stéphanie Pauline Nathalie [Foucault]."

80. *Almanach parisien, ou Liste des 55 000 principaux habitans de Paris. Suivi d'une table des rues pour l'année 1828,* 2d year (Paris: Chez les éditeurs, rue des Marais-du-Temple, n° 14, 1828).

81. "Lettre de Pierre-François-Victor Foucault à Son Altesse Eminentissime Mgr. le Prince de Croÿ, Cardinal et Grand

Aumônier de France, le 4 juillet 1828. . . , Dossier personnel de Foucault (Thérèse-Adèle)," MS Archives des Quinze-Vingts P48/3506; "Certificat d'incurabilité pour M. Foucault, établi par le docteur Legras, médecin du 6e dispensaire, le 25 février 1830, Dossier personnel de Foucault (Thérèse-Adèle)," MS Archives des Quinze-Vingts P48/3506; "Baptême de Stéphanie Pauline Nathalie [Foucault].

82. *Eliza, ou Le Modèle de la piété filiale, suivi de Le Bienfaiteur inconnu et Le Premier emploi de l'argent; Les Trois sœurs, ou Les Effets de l'aveuglement maternel; La Maison dans les bois, ou La Famille vertueuse; Les soirées récréatives d'un curé de campagne;* and *Mélanie, ou Les Suites de l'ingratitude, suivi des Deux aveugles, ou Souvenirs d'illustres émigrés.*

83. Lejeune-Resnick, "Les Femmes écrivains," 99.

84. Ibid., 105.

85. Madame Foucault née Husson, *Le Passe-temps moral, ou La Vertu mise en action,* 2d ed. (Paris: Belin–Le Prieur, Libraire, 1832), Préface.

86. Geoffroy de Grandmaison, *La Congrégation (1801–1830)* (Paris: Librairie Plon, 1889), 219–20; Guillaume de Bertier de Sauvigny, *Une Figure d'ultra-royaliste: Le comte Ferdinand de Bertier (1782–1864) et l'énigme de la Congrégation* (Paris: Les Presses continentales, 1948), 58–60.

87. Lyons, *Le Triomphe du livre,* 12, 14.

88. Société Catholique des Bons Livres, *Association pour la Formation des dépôts de Bons livres* (Paris: Imprimerie ecclésiastique de Béthune, imprimeur de la Société Catholique des Bons Livres, n.d.), 6–8.

89. Abbé Perreau was on the Administrative Council of this association while the cardinal Prince de Croÿ, Grand Chaplain of France, was the association's protector with the Duc de Rivière, who was then the president of both the Catholic Society for Worthy Books and the Society for Worthy Learning (he succeeded to the Duc de Montmorency, who died in April 1826).

The Duc de Rivière had also succeeded Mathieu de Montmorency as the administrative governor of the Quinze-Vingts.

90. "Déclarations des imprimeurs parisiens, Registres pour les années 1826, 1828 (juillet-décembre) et 1829 (juillet–décembre)," MS Archives Nationales F18 II 13, 16, 18; Lejeune-Resnick, "Les Femmes écrivains," 95-96.

91. The Arrondissement numbers refer to the system used before 1859.

92. Bureau de Charité du 10e arrondissement, "Extrait du Livre des Pauvres, le 26 février 1830, Dossier personnel de Foucault (Pierre-François)," MS Archives des Quinze-Vingts, P48/3504.

93. "Certificat d'incurabilité pour Mme Foucault, établi par le docteur Legras, le 25 février 1830, Dossier personnel de Foucault (Thérèse-Adèle)," MS Archives des Quinze-Vingts, P48/3506.

94. Ibid.

95. "Baptême de Marie Geneviève Elisa [Foucault]."

96. Bureau de charité du 4e arrondissement (ancien) de Paris, "Délibérations 1816–1832, 6e Registre, du 25 novembre 1829 au 27 octobre 1831, Séance du 4 août 1830, Inscription au rôle des pauvres: n° 5123, Foucault, François Victor; Admission aux Secours spéciaux, Aveugles: n° 39 Foucault, Pierre-François-Victor, rue de Sartine, n° 2; n° 40 Fe Foucault, Thérèse-Adèle Husson, rue de Sartine, n° 2," MS Archives de l'Assistance Publique-Hôpitaux de Paris, FOSS 162.

97. "Lettre de Pierre-François-Victor Foucault à Son Altesse Eminentissime Mgr le Prince de Croÿ, Cardinal et Grand Aumônier de France, le 4 juillet 1828, Note liminaire, Dossier personnel de Foucault (Thérèse-Adèle)," MS Archives des Quinze-Vingts, P48/3506.

98. Hôtel-Dieu, "Registre des entrées du 1er janvier au 31 mars 1831," MS Archives de l'Assistance Publique-Hôpitaux de Paris, 1Q2 145; and Hôtel-Dieu, "Registre des décès, Année

1831," MS Archives de l'Assistance Publique-Hôpitaux de Paris, 3Q2 34.

99. "Registre destiné à recueillir les délibérations et arrêtés de l'administration des Quinze-Vingts, par notre administrateur provisoire de cet hospice, du 5 septembre 1831 au 24 juin 1835; 14 novembre 1832, Permission de mariage accordée au Sr Foucault par l'administration," MS Archives des Quinze-Vingts.

100. "Admission de Foucaux (Pierre-François-Victor), Registre des admissions du 15 octobre 1829 à avril 1845," MS Archives des Quinze-Vingts.

101. Edgar Guilbeau, *Chants et légendes de l'aveugle* (Paris: L. Boulanger éditeur, 1891), 49.

102. Quoted in Bricard, *Saintes ou pouliches*, 98.

103. Announcements ran in *La Quotidienne* and the *Journal des Dames et des Modes* in October 1827.

104. The play was first performed at the Théâtre Français on December 21, 1822, and would prove to be one of Scribe's most frequently produced plays at the Comédie Française during the entire nineteenth century, with 393 shows from 1822 to 1874. One knockoff was *Valérien, ou Le Jeune aveugle* [Valérien, or The Blind Youth], a melodrama in two acts by Carrion-Nisas and Sauvage; it was staged on April 17, 1823, at the Théâtre de la Porte Saint-Martin. Two burlesque parodies, *M. Oculi, ou La Cataracte* [Mr. Oculi, or The Cataract] by Désaugiers and Adolphe came to the Théâtre des Variétés in January 1823, and *La Cataracte* [The Cataract] by Dupin and Varner was performed at the Gymnasium the following February. We thank M. Jean-Claude Yon, maître de conférences at the Université de Versailles-Saint-Quentin en Yvelines, for this information on the history of *Valérie* at the Comédie Française.

105. Rodenbach did the same when he published his *Lettre sur les aveugles faisant suite à celle de Diderot* [Letter on the Blind Following That of Diderot]: "By A. Rodenbach, blind, member of the Museum for the Blind of Paris."

About the Authors

Catherine J. Kudlick is an associate professor of history at the University of California, Davis, and the author of *Cholera in Post-Revolutionary Paris: A Cultural History.* Dr. Zina Weygand is a researcher at the Laboratoire Brigitte Frybourg pour L'Insertion Sociale des Personnes Handicapées at the Conservatoire Nationale des Arts et Métiers in Paris and is the author of numerous articles on the history of blind people in France. Thérèse-Adèle Husson (1803–1831) was the author of numerous novels and essays published in mid-nineteenth-century Paris.